DIVING FOR NORTHWEST RELICS

Identification and Dating of Bottles, Pottery and Marine Hardware

By James Seeley White

Diving for Northwest Relics takes the reader on a tour through the collection of ships' relics, bottles, and pottery that have been gathered primarily by one diver, the author. It is an example of what an individual, with knowledge, equipment, and an adventurous spirit, can learn from marks left by those who passed through our waterways before us. It is intended to assist others who would like to explore those regions, and understand what they encounter there.

In the Pacific Northwest, early travelers and settlers were dependent upon the sea and the rivers as their primary transportation routes. Along these watery paths they left reminders of their passing—often the bottles and other discards that are collectors' items of today. Sea captains and sailors also contributed their unique additions to the residue on the river and harbor floors. Some of these objects have a distinct nautical flavor, like the glassware and pottery designed for shipboard use or transport by sea.

While the majority of relics to be found by divers relates to everyday life on the waterways, the most thrilling discoveries are associated with the ships that plied the waters. Shipwrecks provide fascinating finds, primarily to the fortunate few who are first on the scene after the salvors have ceased their labors, or to those who stumble upon an obscure hulk that is fully abandoned. Even larger numbers of ships' relics are to be found where they were accidentally dropped near repair docks, and at locations where cleaning and painting took place while the vessels awaited cargo or passengers. Special equipment, such as underwater metal detectors, helps the diver interested in treasure hunting. Knowledge of techniques further increases the odds of a thrilling find.

D1372256

Relic diving in one section of Nehalem Bay, Oregon, produced this 24-inch propeller, mast-light lens, compass, and many old bottles. These examples are (left to right): W.J. Van Schuyver, Portland, whiskey bottle; another of different style; North Pacific Brewery, Astoria, Oregon; Enterprise Brewing Co., San Francisco, California; and Pacific Soda Works, Tillamook, Oregon.

DIVING FOR NORTHWEST RELICS

Identification and Dating of
Bottles, Pottery and Marine Hardware

By James Seeley White

Binford & Mort
Thomas Binford, Publisher

2536 S.E. Eleventh • Portland, Oregon 97202

CONTENTS

INTRODUCTION

The paraphernalia of the sea has always fascinated me, even as a child. Tales of shipwreck and treasure were among my favorite reading. As an adult I found myself in a shore-bound career, but ventured onto the waterways at every opportunity and eventually became a boat owner.

Eighteen years ago, some friends introduced me to the sport of scuba diving. Soon afterward I discovered that nautical objects which had fascinated me could occasionally be picked up from the ocean and river floors. Other friends showed me where best to seek these items, and introduced me to the metal detectors and other equipment that made the search easier. Because I have shared in the diving experiences of others throughout the Pacific Northwest—Oregon, Washington, British Columbia, and northern California—I would now like to pass on to others some of the experiences and knowledge I have gained.

In *Diving for Northwest Relics* I have attempted to describe categories of collectable objects from the waterways in sufficient detail that others may be able to determine the identity and approximate age of their own discoveries. Material has been gathered from old catalogs, directories, reference books, and through correspondence with experts in order to assemble this information. However, the most important background for this book has been the actual experiences of frustration, occasional danger, and discovery. There is no substitute for this personal knowledge.

The first part of *Diving for Northwest Relics* deals with items related to the ships that plied our waterways: compasses, propellers, anchors, lights, ports, and related matter. Shared in this section are some of the most thrilling finds in my diving experience. The second part is written especially for my diving friends who have found an interest in glassware of the waters, and have often asked how to tell the age of a bottle and what it was used for. They have the opportunity to gather fascinating glass and pottery containers, objects like the white pottery import beer bottles and the black glass ales that sailors tossed overboard. There have been few reference works on this subject. I hope to help fill that void.

In a third section, a new interest in objects from the waterways may be introduced to many. This part deals with the long-neglected subject of chinaware and pottery associated with shipping. Seagoing pottery, after all, did have its differences. Finally, some of my personal thoughts on the quest—and how I will follow it in the future—are presented. Places to be explored and equipment to be used, are discussed. I hope to meet you out there someday; there is plenty of room for all of us.

DIVING FOR
NORTHWEST RELICS

Identification and Dating of
Bottles, Pottery and Marine Hardware

PART I.
SHIP RELICS FROM NORTHWEST WATERS

CHAPTER 1.

ANCHORS, PROPELLERS, AND WHEELS — SYMBOLS OF SEAFARING

Anchors

It was in the San Juan Islands of Washington that I ran into them, a group of young men totally exhausted. They had stumbled upon an old anchor beneath the sea, and followed its chain to the bitter end. Their minds had whirled with thoughts of shipwreck booty and cannons, perhaps even a bit of gold. They were sure a shipwreck must be just beyond the area they had searched, and had ceased their efforts only as darkness and exhaustion overtook them. Doggedly, they returned the next day, but no hulk was found.

The presence of an anchor doesn't necessarily mean a ship was wrecked near that site. True, if a ship did go down it probably had at least one anchor with it, or was dragging one when swept to its death on the rocks or shoals. However, nearly every harbor has yielded anchors that were lost when couplings broke, or when rigging slipped as a replacement was being slung. Most vessels carried spare anchors; some had more than one type aboard, and used different ones for differing purposes.

Wreck diving has always been thrilling, often the high point of adventure, but, of the many anchors I have discovered, none have been associated with a shipwreck. This has not detracted from their intrinsic value, though, for the anchor is symbolic of all that is nautical—a spirit carried on Navy buttons, yachting flags, caps, and monograms.

1

Occasionally one finds an old anchor exposed among the rocks. Others seem to come and go—exposed one year by scouring wave or flood action, then hidden away again by shifting sands. Our greatest success has been by swimming along the channels carved by the whims of ocean or river currents. At Yaquina City, Oregon, my diving partner and I each were surprised by the discovery of the anchors that grace our dens. A third anchor was located with an underwater metal detector. Detectors seem infallible on large masses like anchors.

We were at first delighted to find the third anchor, one much larger than the previous two, but also made with curved flukes and a crossbar ending in large iron balls. However, we could not even begin to lift it from where we traced its shape in the mud by the metal-detector readings. We thought of attaching lift bags and inflating them, rounding up all the buddies we could for the real gut effort of dragging it to shore and up the bank, but finally decided to leave it where it was. We each had a more-practical-sized anchor, and were thinking of all the work to save them after they were out of the water.

Old anchors were made of iron, and iron rusts away. Over the course of a century of salt water, the flukes of a fifty-pound or sixty-pound anchor may be almost rusted through. Much of what is seen is actually iron oxide, a substance that will shrink, crack, and fall off if not treated. (My anchor from Yaquina City was thought to have been a fifty-pounder, but weighed only thirty-eight when dried.)

The first step I went through in saving my anchor was to clean off the material that detracted from its appearance (mud, but not all the nicer barnacles and worm tubes). Salt from sea water had to be extracted by soaking the anchor in fresh water, with frequent changes, for about a month. Then, the drying and cracking was reduced by soaking the relic in ethylene glycol. This replaces the water, inhibits further rust, and is compatible with the protective coating (water is not). The remaining step was the binder and protective coating of fiberglass.

Polyester resin can be painted onto the relic once it has the water removed by ethylene glycol and drying. The resin should be catalyzed lightly enough to allow time to soak in before hardening; it may even be thinned with a little (very little) acetone.

The last step took several months. The preserving job was not perfect, so some cracks developed. These were treated by pouring in more fiberglass as a filler and binder. Finally, the anchor was protected and the odor of decaying marine life effectively sealed off.

This same method can be used on other iron-oxide items. The exterior will be preserved and have a glossy, wet appearance. Brittleness remains, though, and in severely rusted objects the thin, brittle shell of fiberglass will be all that holds the trophy together. At one time a "peavey" head (metal tip of a lever used for handling logs) hung on my workshop wall. It was a souvenir of a dive beneath a former ferry landing where loggers had arrived and departed from the cutting area on Washington's Olympic Peninsula near Brinnon. Commuting had taken place across Hood Canal from the sawmill town of Seabeck. The handle of the log-rolling tool had long since been consumed by marine borers, but the iron point and C-shaped hook remained. It was interesting enough to warrant preservation with fiberglass.

My trophy hung there until the day I decided to add a tool rack to the wall. Then, jarred loose by the hammering, it fell to the concrete floor and shattered into hundreds of pieces, as though it had been made of glass.

Propellers

In my estimation, propellers are even more exciting finds than anchors, and are less frequently encountered. Wrecks are quickly looted of these impressive brass items because of their salvage value. Most often, they are recovered by a contract salvor at the instructions of the owner or the insurance carrier. Only old, abandoned wrecks are fair game for the amateur.

Wreck of the former ANNA FOSS has been visible on the west shore of Vashon Island, Washington, during exceptionally low tides. However, it is rapidly crumbling. It had been retired from service and was awaiting conversion when it sank at anchor.

The blades, hub, shaft, pitch-control rod, seals, and tubes are all of brass in this propeller system from a wrecked steam launch discovered at Corvallis, Oregon. Note the patch on one blade.

e originally thought we had found a piece of modern brass sculpture when this propeller guard was encountered. (Prop was recovered later.)

Blades of this hand-forged brass propeller, recovered by the author from Yaquina Bay, Oregon, were completely oxidized at the edges. Damage inadvertently occurred as he climbed a piling to raise the prize.

Left: Anchor suggestive of the Rodgers type—recovered from the vanished 19th century port of Yaquina City, Oregon—rests in the author's driveway. Right: When this 24-inch brass propeller was found in Nehalem Bay, no line was available and it was too heavy to swim with. It was brought out by climbing up the slippery bank under water.

Left: This small-craft wheel, found in American Lake, Washington, was thickly coated with iron oxide. Right: After flaking and sanding, the same wheel is ready for fiberglass coating.

The *lost* propeller, on the other hand, is frequently forgotten, and its precise location may not be known. Occasionally a shaft breaks, or the nut loosens from the shaft so propeller and nut back off during reversing. Other props were carried on deck as spares. Vessels working in close proximity to reefs or subject to collison damage (such as tugs moving log rafts and barges) carried extra propellers—almost like the spare tire on the family car. These were sometimes lost in heavy seas or capsizing.

Of course, discovering an old, lost prop is mostly just luck. Last year a companion and I were moving along the bottom of Nehalem Bay, looking for antique bottles, when I spotted the outline of a propeller in the mud. It turned out to be a 24-inch brass prop, probably from a small tug or large fishing boat. It was too heavy to swim with, we had no lift bag along, and, in the murky water of the channel, I feared I would never find it again if I left to get a lift bag or line. My solution was to hoist it onto a shoulder and walk. It was quite a trek, sinking halfway to my knees with each step toward the nearest bank, then on my knees and one hand as I struggled up the slippery incline.

That prop weighed thirty-five pounds and was about heavy enough for me. Ships' propellers present almost insurmountable lifting problems for the non-professional, for they weigh anywhere from a few hundred pounds to several tons. If one is a collector of marine relics, a further problem is what to do with something so heavy once it has been recovered. From the purely collecting standpoint, it seems reasonable to confine the fun to locating and bringing home propellers of sizes found on small tugs, fishing boats, and small craft. The larger ones are best left to the professional salvors.

One caution with old props: they aren't as sturdy as they might appear. Casting of propellers is an art almost of this century. Many of the 19th century were of iron and not much value, and even the early brass ones were forged—heated and hammered into shape. Such brass is subject to flaws and may appear layered in composition, thus being more prone to oxidation in salt water. I found such an old prop near the dock area at Newport, Oregon, and shinnied up a piling to get it up to the dive boat. To my dismay, the edges of the old brass propeller were deeply chipped; portions of the blades were oxidized clear through.

On the other hand, fresh water is kind to brass. A variable-pitch propeller system removed from a 26-ft. steam launch found in the Willamette River near Corvallis, Oregon, was still in excellent condition except for the iron parts. A little scrubbing and polishing revealed hammer and file marks from its hand-made origin.

Wheels

The rarest of nautical trophies is the ship's wooden steering wheel. This desirable relic is made of many pieces of select hardwood fitted together in a traditional shape. Unfortunately, this lovely wood is quickly attacked by borers if the ship settles in salt water. By the time salvage efforts are abandoned, or an old wreck is discovered, this wooden wheel suffers irreparable damage.

Fresh water, of course, contains no borers. My wheel discoveries have been confined to vessels that have gone down into our rivers and lakes, and fortune has confined even these to small craft. Of the older small craft, like the 26-ft. steam launch near Corvallis, the wheels were not attractive enough to retain as relics. The steering apparatus of the launch (much to my disappointment) consisted of a horizontal wooden spool over which the line flowed as on a capstan. At one end of the spool was an iron wheel. The whole thing was very simple, and very rusted.

In American Lake, Washington, Geary Hughes, Carole Bentley, and I recovered a small-craft wheel that appeared very corroded but cleaned up nicely. Much to Carole's later regret, she passed up a similar wheel because of its apparent condition and the work required. It just didn't look worth the effort at the time.

Pacific Mail Steamship Co.

NEW YORK LINE via PANAMA.

Steamships HENRY CHAUNCEY, OCEAN QUEEN, RISING STAR, MONTANA, ARIZONA, CONSTITUTION — Side Wheel,
3,000 Tons each.

COLIMA, ACAPULCO, COLON, GRANADA, COSTA RICA, MONTANA,
Iron Screw, 2,500 Tons each.

Leave New York 10th, 20th, 30th. Leave San Francisco every **Seventeenth Day**,
for the East, commencing January 7th, at 12 o'clock noon.

SAN DIEGO BRANCH.

Steamers ORIZABA, PACIFIC, SENATOR, MOHONGO — Iron Side Wheel,
2,000 Tons.

Leave San Francisco every **Saturday**, at **10 A. M.**, for Santa Barbara.
San Pedro and San Diego.

CHINA LINE.

Steamers CHINA, COLORADO, GREAT REPUBLIC, JAPAN, ALASKA,
Side Wheel, 4,500 Tons each.

(YOKOHAMA and HONGKONG, Iron Screws, 5,000 Tons each, building,)

Leave San Francisco on the 1st of every Month, at 12 o'clock noon, for Hongkong,
Via Yokohama, Japan.

SHANGHAE BRANCH.

Steamers GOLDEN AGE, OREGONIAN, NEW YORK, COSTA RICA, ARIEL
and RELIEF — Side Wheel, 2,500 Tons,

Leave Yokohama for Shanghae via Inland Sea of Japan, calling at Hiogo and
Nagasaki four times a month, and for Hakodate on
the 1st of every month.

☞ When Sailing dates fall on Sunday, steamer will leave preceding Saturday.

Office of the Company in San Francisco,
At the WHARF, cor. First and Brannan Sts.

The Pacific Mail Steamship Company's 1870 ship roster includes several tragic sources of relics of the deep. The *PACIFIC* went down off Cape Flattery on the night of Nov. 4, 1875, with a loss of 275 lives. The *OREGONIAN* was wrecked at the Coquille River bar on Jan. 16, 1877; the *GREAT REPUBLIC* rammed into Sand Island on the Columbia River in April, 1879, and the *ALASKA* was wrecked in the Farallon Islands in September of the same year. (The *ALASKA* was later salvaged.)

I am aware of only a few really nice wooden wheels recovered from Northwest waters. Most were obtained from commercial divers who removed them from sunken vessels. Such is usually the case, for these would be taken as part of the salvage operation.

CHAPTER 2.

BRASS AND GLASS

Special characteristics are required for metal to survive centuries, even just decades, in salt water. Electrolysis speeds deterioration—usually called rust—in metal but with varying rates in different metals, and with dissimilar circumstances. Gold is one of the most corrosion-resistant metals, but little of that is lying around waiting for the average diver. On the other hand, many items found on ships are made of brass and copper, two of the next most corrosion-resistant materials. And, like gold, brass will often take on a shiny, yellow finish after long exposure to salt water.

As noted, different metals decompose at differing rates. Aluminum is one of the metals most rapidly deteriorating in salt water, zinc more rapidly than iron or steel, then nickel, tin, and lead. Brass, copper, and silver last longer, and here is an interesting observation: these metals survive best if in contact with one of the more readily decomposed metals like iron. The electrolysis has its greatest effect on the more susceptible metal, sparing the resistant. Brass valves survive with a fine finish while their iron handles are eaten away. Silver coins are preserved if in contact with copper pennies.

Another observation is that smaller or thinner parts are destroyed first. The first brass compass I found was in Oregon's Siletz River. We had given up finding a fishing vessel that had sunk and been carried away by a flood about ten years earlier. We were drifting with the current, picking up fishing lures

11

when, suddenly, there the compass was, sitting upright and intact on the bottom. Some water had seeped into the turpentine in the bowl. (This one wasn't filled with the usual ethyl alcohol and probably was made during prohibition.) Although all else was solid, the small brass bolts that secured the sealing ring crumbled at the gentlest touch. In fact, the pieces were cleaned out of the threaded holes in the base by twirling a pin in the threads. The brass combination light from the wreck was the same way—bolts crumbled, allowing the larger sections to fall apart.

Glass is a frequent companion material in brass objects, and also stoutly resists deterioration in the sea. In fact, the determining criterion as to whether glass will decompose is not moisture but the minerals in the mud where the glass has lain. Because of this, glassware found in separate geographic locations shows distinct characterists in the amount of surface etching. We were disappointed with the cloudy surfaces of the bottles found in Heriot Bay, British Columbia, when compared to bottles of similar age removed from Nehalem Bay, Oregon.

Glass is impervious to marine borers. It can be soaked overnight in a strong solution of laundry bleach and detergent, and most of the encrustations wipe away. Generally speaking, brass and glass items make up some of the nicest relics to be found in the sea.

Compasses

Perhaps the most sought-after trophy of brass and glass is the ship's compass. While the anchor has been symbolic of the sailor's trade, and the propeller a reminder of the power that thrust mighty ships through the waves, the compass is known for the preciseness of navigation that guided vessels across trackless oceans. The value of discovered relics of this type has soared in recent years. Few are available on the market, so they are difficult to appraise; one appraisal may be quite unlike another. Those given for my favorite compass have varied by hundreds of dollars.

So far, none of the compasses in my collection have been plucked from the bulkheads of dead ships. It is true that the first one found, the compass from the Siletz River, was part of the wreckage of a broken-up vessel, but it was completely out by itself when found.

The compass that surprised me most I found at Quadra Island, British Columbia. I had no idea of finding any ship's relics as we started the dive. The water was so clear I had a feeling of flying as I more glided than swam to the gravelly ocean floor I could so clearly see below. Sculpins darted off and cockle clams closed their shells as I first touched bottom. The natural setting was interrupted by scattered beer bottles—obviously, numerous craft had passed over these waters.

As I drifted along with the current, peering into clumps of eelgrass and occasionally picking up a bottle to consider its worth, I came upon a few cups and dishes. One plate was a Wedgewood-blue English Countryside design, so I placed it in my sack. Nearby, I noticed an upright bowl-like object with a balancing ring around the top. Curious, I wiped the silt from the flat lid—and looked with amazement through the glass to the handpainted card of a fluid-filled mariner's compass.

My initial thought was that the compass had been accidentally dropped from one of the vessels that regularly moored there. I showed it and inquired nearby, but thanks to the honesty of a number of Canadians, no one claimed it. Later, in researching its past, I learned the compass was made in the late 19th century and must have lain on the bottom for some time. It is likely that both the Wedgewood dish and the compass were lost in some forgotten capsizing.

A third compass was discovered in much the same way. We were looking about in Nehalem Bay where the fireboat had tied up at Wheeler, Oregon. The water wasn't very clear; it never is around Wheeler, but we could see large objects fifteen feet away. I had picked up an interesting pop bottle and a brass fire nozzle, and was about ready to swim up and look for our boat, when I noticed a square in the mud. Scooping down with my fingers, I came up with the four sides of a mahogany box and the compass it contained. I carefully cradled it in my hands and headed up for the inflatable.

Telescopes

Like compasses, telescopes carry the mystic image of guiding ships home from the sea. Their uses included helping identify headlands once a landfall has been made, and locating the channel entrance to a harbor. Such treasurers I would not expect to find intact under water, however. Corrosion would long ago have destroyed the thin tubes, for telescopes were replaced with binoculars 50 years ago. Mine are from trading and purchasing.

The oldest telescope in my collection was purchased from Roy Harwood at the Nehalem Bay Trading Company. He obtained it from the family of a sea captain who had sailed in and out of the Seattle area. It has four extendible brass tubes that slide within the main body, and when fully drawn is slightly over 40 inches (1 meter) in length. Originally, the main tube was covered with black leather, but this had become brittle and flaked away. A brass cap still protects the objective lens when not in use; an internal disc that swings aside when the telescope is rotated protects the eyepiece. It appears to have about 30 power.

In style, this old telescope that once served on Northwest waters is European. European manufacture is also a sound assumption on the basis that America was dependent on foreign sources for high quality optical glass until around 1912. No markings are to be found, but it was not unusual for the maker's marks to be engraved on the smallest draw tube near the eyepiece, a place where years of wear might obliterate them. It was also not until the Tariff Act of 1891 that the country of manufacture was required to be stamped into such products, and this telescope could easily pre-date that act.

Another telescope in my collection has a single draw tube, extending the overall length to 22 inches (54 cm). It is obviously

The ship's clock (left), discovered at Rock Bay, British Columbia, crumbled at the slightest touch. On the other hand, a gold-plated railroad watch (right), with the most recent patent date on the works shown as 1910, was solid and gleaming when found in the channel of Nehalem Bay, Oregon.

A covering of soft mud prevented marine borers from destroying the sides of the mahogany case for the compass on the left, recovered from Nehalem Bay. It was used as a pattern to restore the one on the right, found in the Siletz. (*Treasure Found* photo)

Left: A ship's compass, measuring a little over 8 inches (21 cm) across, between the far points of the gimbals, is shown where it lay on the floor of a cove near Campbell River, British Columbia. It continued to function, though a layer of algae and silt obscured the card in this photo. Right: This ship's compass has been my favorite discovery. The compass card is hand painted, the sealing ring hand drilled and attached to the base. Terence Elworthy, Director of the Vancouver Maritime Museum, wrote me that A.P.W. Williamson—whose name appears on the compass—was a deep-water Master Mariner who settled in early Vancouver, B.C., and started a nautical book and instrument shop. In subsequent ownerships, the shop has been R.F. Bovey, Ltd., and most recently, The Quarterdeck.

Six-year-old daughter, Mimmie, can almost hide behind the pile of brass ports collected during one of the author's better days of diving. They were from a wooden ship whose cabin and hull were eaten away, leaving the ports easily removed, some fallen out.

newer. On the draw tube are the markings, "U.S. NAVY Officer of the Deck," the power rating of 12-1/2 and the imprint of the Bausch & Lomb Optical Company. Instead of the swinging protective disc at the eyepiece of the older telescope, this one has a yellow filter to aid vision in foggy conditions. The filter swings out of view when the telescope is rotated, just like the black protective disc. Brown leather sheathing is stitched in place over the main tube.

According to Ronald J. Eisen, Director of Corporate Communications of Bausch & Lomb, the telescope was manufactured by their company between 1908 and 1916. A small z in the telescope's markings refers to an association with the Carl Zeiss Optical Works in Germany, a relationship that ended with World War I.

Like the larger of the telescopes, I purchased the U.S. Navy scope. It was obtained from a neighbor, a man retired from the sea, whose father had purchased the telescope from a sailor in Aberdeen, Washington, and passed it on to him. Both telescopes are in good condition. The older of the two recently saw duty again, accompanying me aboard my boat, the JUNE Q, during a cruise through British Columbia waters.

My collection has a few more brass items that I have purchased or traded for rather than found. These are flare pistols, obtained from several sources. The largest, made entirely of brass except for the springs, was intended to fire large (37mm) parachute flares. It was manufactured during World War II, and could be used at the scene of a sinking to provide a large amount of light. The gun was made by SKLAR, Los Angeles, California, and the flares for it by International Flare Signal Division of Kilgore Mfg., Tipp City, Ohio.

The most interesting one has a brass frame with a trigger spur, and a short 10-gauge shotgun barrel. It is stamped on the barrel, "MARK III, The Remington Arms-Union Metalic Cartridge Co., Inc." When I obtained it, somewhat damaged, I wrote to Remington concerning replacement parts and the history of the gun. The company representative wrote back to state that it was a World War I flare pistol, and to caution me not to use 10-gauge shotgun shells in it. The chamber would accept the shells, but the gun was not designed to withstand the recoil. No wonder it had a bent frame and cracked grip. Someone must have had a real sore hand!

A third flare pistol is not brass, but is made of an aluminum alloy. It is a standard U.S. Navy flare gun of World War II, and uses a flare cartridge similar in size to a 10-gauge shotgun shell. Mine is marked U S N and SIGNAL PISTOL MARK 5, D.F. Sedgeley Inc., 1943.

Port Lights

One of the most spectacular rises in value in marine relics has been the collector's price of a brass port light (commonly referred to on shore as a porthole). Technically, the porthole is the hole in the ship, through which air and light are admitted, or through which a cannon is fired. The brass frame and round glass window is a port light. It is usually hinged to an encircling flange which serves as the attachment to the ship. A second hinged item that may be present is a heavy metal disc, called a deadlight, which is secured against the inside of the port in rough weather, cutting out all light and ventilation, but also keeping the sea out should the glass of the port light be broken. Fixtures, even without the deadlight—that originally sold for $25 apiece when new—now bring ten times that amount in antique and collector shops. This seems astounding when one considers the number of port lights on a ship, and the number of ships that have gone to the dismantling yards. Still, the demand continues—and grows.

This high value has resulted in fierce competition among wreck divers to gain possession of the port lights. Often, laws of ownership and salvage are violated by over-eager individuals who do not wait for a vessel to be truly abandoned. Others take unwarranted risks to snatch relics from wreckages that have come to rest in continuously hazardous waters. Only a few have been as fortunate as one diver acquaintance who, while spear-fishing on the northern Washington coast, happened upon the wreckage of a wooden-hulled vessel. The timber of the hull had long since been reduced by borers and rot, leaving the brass port lights and other items simply to be picked up.

A few years ago, I had a similar experience. I went down to retrieve a friend's dropped tools and came upon a brass port light lying on the bottom. Others were nearby, parts of the residue of a fallen-apart wooden ship. Several thrilling days were spent searching through the debris, accumulating brass fittings. One of those days proved to be my most productive in terms of brass ports recovered. My score that day was seven—four 21 inches (52 cm) across the flange, and three small examples 10-1/2 inches (27 cm) in overall width. The only thing that marred the experience was that, in my eagerness, I pulled a muscle in my back; the port lights weighed 50 lbs. (24 kilograms) each and I tried to pull up two at once. Oh, well, I was grinning as I rubbed my aching back.

The ports gathered in this experience were obviously designed for mounting on a wooden hull. The flanges were drilled and countersunk for 5/16-inch wood screws. The thick glass of the port lights was also of greenish hue similar to the coloration of many 19th century patent medicine bottles. When battened to the flange, they were held shut by four lugs, except for a few from which two lugs had been cut away. Two holding lugs are much less cumbersome, so most later port lights were made for only that number.

Port lights from steel-hulled vessels tend to be constructed for only two lugs to batten down, usually have clear glass, and are recognizable by the larger-diameter holes in the flange where they were attached to the steel side of the ship by bolts. Many are not of brass, but were fabricated of galvanized steel.

I am aware of a few port lights that are still to be removed from shipwrecks. However, one of the locations is in the side of a crumbling wooden vessel—the side that is thrust down into the mud of the dismal depths. Another is in the surf line of a tumultuous coast. Neither are locations that I frequently dive, though I have ventured on both wrecks.

In a few instances port lights break loose from a wreck and wave action carries them to shore. A few winters ago, Bob Loeffel of Newport, Oregon, was beachcombing near Seal Rock and came upon a large brass port. In another lucky incident, children fishing from a dock in Gig Harbor, Washington, tangled their fishing line on something on the bottom, and drew up a small galvanized port.

Ships' Lights

For lovers of things nautical, one of the most impressive sights is watching a ship slide by on a placid waterway at night. Whether it is accompanied by the far-off clumping sound of a propeller-driven freighter, or the silent gliding past of sail, there is something mystic about the movement. All seems peaceful and orderly, an experience heightened by the bright lights that mark the vessel. Perhaps it is the reaction to these lights that makes a collector treasure the ship's lighting apparatus, and the diver thrill at finding such items at the bottom of the sea. Both the running and anchor lights that marked the ship to other mariners, and the lights that lighted the companionways and cabins are eagerly sought.

I well remember the delight of finding my first running light, a brass combination light from the same Siletz River wreck that gave me my first compass. Although the light is from a mere fishing craft, it still rates a place of honor in my study.

At Nehalem, Oregon, we anticipated finding more lights. When we first found the area and were grubbing a wide assortment of relics from the mud around the old dock location, we had high hopes. I first dug out a couple of dark green starboard light lenses, then two large, clear anchor light lenses. These latter items could well have dated from the days of sail, for both contained bubbles in the glass, and one had been carefully hand ground to fit its lamp. However, none of our mud-poking turned up the metal parts of a running light. Most such relics

Left: This light, with brass base and frame, blue-green and red lenses, is a running light. Right: This port-side light is constructed of galvanized sheet metal and has soldered seams, a method of joining that was seldom used after 1920.

Left: The smaller lamp was spotted during a dive in Gowland Harbor, British Columbia; the matching chimney came from Gig Harbor, Washington. The tall lamp was recovered from the channel near Nehalem. Right: This masthead light was uncovered in an old barn near Astoria, Oregon. It was lighted by a kerosene lamp inserted into the hole in the base.

The electric light on the left was recovered from a sunken tug.
The kerosene lamp is from a stern light.

Left: Water-level gauge (center) was removed from the engine room of a wrecked tug. The C-shaped object is a brass fitting found at the site of a steamer explosion near Butteville, Oregon. Right: The author examines what appears to be a steam whistle he had just found.
(Photo courtesy of Treasure Magazine)

were made of sheet metal coated with zinc, and apparently, through the years, salt water had destroyed the metal parts.

After a time we left the Nehalem dock area and drifted with the current along other channels in the bay. Although our searches revealed wrecks of several sizes, no lighting artifacts turned up in any of them. Instead, all of our lighting objects from Nehalem were apparently lost overboard, perhaps while cleaning or refilling the founts (fuel containers).

Interior lighting is also fascinating. Some kerosene lamps were gimbaled—set in pivoting rings that let them turn so they would remain upright despite the ship's roll. I was particularly intrigued with a glass lamp of the type sometimes called a trawler's lamp, that I found on the floor of Gowland Harbor, British Columbia. Unfortunately, it was missing an appropriate chimney. Years later, as I was preparing to drop beneath the surface of Gig Harbor, Washington, I was told by my host, "You might find some Canadian things down there, for a lot of Canadian vessels used to call here." And, it was there, near the base of a piling, that I found a chimney which matched my lamp.

From the numbers I have found at the bottom of seaports, I am inclined to think that some lamps very similar to household ones may have been used in cabins during calm periods, and in inland waterways. Such kerosene lamps have been found in the Alsea and Nehalem bays in Oregon and among the Discovery Islands of the British Columbia coast.

As shipping entered the 20th century vessels also entered the age of electricity. Fixtures of the early days were much different from what is in use today, and many confusing relics lie on the floors of our waterways. Most commonly found are the ceramic bases of electrical receptacles. Switches were often of the throw type, with a brass lever ending in a hard black rubber handle. The brass lever made contact between two brass prongs mounted on a rectangular ceramic base. These white blocks, about 1-3/4 inches (2 cm) wide, about the same thickness, and a little over 3 inches (8 cm) long, are often encountered around dock areas. In some commercial fishing communities new switches of this type can still be purchased.

Voltage in the first electrical systems was not standard. Many used 32-volt current and rated their generators on how many 20-watt lights they would power. Others utilized 8, 10, 20, 40, or 115 volts. Some searchlights were designed for 125 volts. The lack of interchangeability was confusing, and the chandlers had to stock a variety of light bulbs with different bases and for all manner of systems. Bulbs were made to several voltages, like 110-125 volts or 28-32 volts. One little ceramic receptacle we found in Nehalem Bay carries an embossed "125 V" but has a threaded brass base too small to accept our familiar Christmas-tree light bulbs.

Of further bewilderment to the collector, conversion kits were introduced to convert kerosene lamps to electricity. When Roy Harwood loaned me his 1918 Oregon Marine & Fisheries Supply catalog, I was surprised to see electrical fixtures shaped like kerosene burners I had found. These, however, were intended to fit in place of the coal-oil lamps of existing running and anchor lights.

The most impressive electrical-system relics we uncovered in our diving were the Edison cells. Unlike the battery of the modern automotive and marine engine, early sea-going electrical units were based on a series of individual cells. (Batteries, by definition, are a series of cells.) In the beginning, a number of white ceramic crocks containing wet cells were lined up to form the electric-power reservoir. For our modern car battery, the cells are in adjoining compartments of a black box.

The Edison Primary Cell consisted of a zinc positive plate, a copper-oxide negative plate, caustic soda electrolyte, and some oil floated on top of the caustic soda solution to prevent evaporation. It has been these ceramic crocks, matching lids, and "Special Battery Oil" bottles of the Edison cells that delighted us in dives from southern Oregon to the passages of British Columbia. They were obviously widely used.

As present times approached, construction styles dictated built-in fixtures. Running lights were build into some wooden vessels. This is the case with the JUNETTA, once an early-day excursion boat, and still a working tug for Neptune Construction Company of Scappoose, Oregon. When she is finally scrapped or lost, collectors will find the lamp lenses to be the only thing of interest in the electrical line.

Other Brass Objects

I have found brass-and-glass items left in engine rooms of presumably salvaged wrecks. A few years ago when a friend introduced me to a favorite wreck, he apologized that it had been stripped. "There have been a lot of divers here since the vessel went down," he said, "and I don't think we will find anything to bring back."

We dived down to the cabin railing, though, slipped beneath, then through the hole where a door had been removed, revealing an engine room. As my eyes adjusted to the dim light, I looked over the encrusted diesel and around the adjoining bulkheads. On the bulkhead tanks hung two lovely old brass water-level gauges. Both were of the two-rod type, meaning they had two brass rods to protect the long glass tube through which the level of the fluid was observed by the marine engineer. Electrolysis had severely eaten the iron handles to the valves, but the brass valves themselves, brass protecting rods, and glass tubes all disassembled and cleaned up beautifully. The brass spigot at the bottom works.

In still another wreck, a fishing boat left at the bottom of Yaquina Bay, Oregon, salvors had removed the engine, propeller, and seemingly everything else of value. Still, a brass drip valve, with needle adjustment and glass viewing port, remained in the debris. One doesn't have to be the first one there to find interesting collectables in the engine room. All that is necessary is careful observation.

The old port areas in Nehalem Bay in Oregon produced an unusual group of brass artifacts. The first of this assortment to be exposed in the mud was a French horn. It had lain bare to the elements too long, though, and crumbled at being removed. The story behind this musical instrument will probably never be told. Could it have been a disgusted musician who threw it there because of continued sour notes? Or, was it an angry neighbor, tired of noise? Unless it fell overboard, it got there with pronounced feeling, for it lay in mid-channel.

Other sound instruments of the Nehalem group were related to shipping. Before electrical horns and compressed air sound devices became common, it was the practice on smaller vessels (other than steam-powered) to utilize breath-activated horns or whistles to signal direction of movement and warnings to other craft. One such item that we found was a small brass horn marked, "D.R.G.M., Germany." It, too, had lain in the water may years, and the flared ends of the two trumpets had become paper thin and cracked.

The most thrilling discovery along this line came when I picked up what appeared to be a small steam whistle. Of sturdier material, it was well-preserved. We envisioned it as having come from one of the steam tugs or excursion boats that once plied the Nehalem River. A piece of wood, taken for driftwood, was withdrawn from the threaded end of the brass chamber and discarded. Later, an old catalog pictured this same object as a "Full-tone" whistle "fitted with polished wood mouthpiece." In 1918 their list price was $2.00 each.

Beyond these are myriad objects of brass that remain from collision, fire, catastrophe, or just plain carelessness. The door locks of well-made wooden ships were of brass, as were some of the mooring cleats. Vessels over certain sizes have long been required to carry firefighting equipment; and though the hoses rot away, the brass nozzles and couplings remain. The corner of my shop is littered with couplings, propellers from outboard motors, hoze nozzles, a large propeller nut, and various other things. Some should be cleaned up and polished as relics; others should be sold as scrap.

These wind instruments—once used to signal vessel movements—were recovered from Nehalem Bay.

Marine firefighting equipment is normally made of brass. Extinguishers like those in the background are scattered about our waterways.

CHAPTER 3.

WOODEN SHIPS AND METAL FITTINGS

It is insidious the way they attack. The structure is intact, the planking and bulkheads seemingly solid. But the teredos are there, inside, hidden by layers of seaweed and barnacles and the outer shell of wood the shipwrights had so carefully fitted.

The next time you visit your favorite wreck (perhaps a wooden-hulled sailing ship or an old steamer), after the winter storms have passed, you may find that instead of an impressive hull, great gaps loom in the side, the deck has collapsed within, and the whole thing is falling apart. Reaching down, you pick up the shape of a plank and it crumbles in your hand, honeycombed by borers.

Rigging Parts

Some woods do resist the gnawing jaws of marine organisms. The planking below the water line of the clipper ship WAR HAWK is said to be of Water Cypress from South America. Though the vessel burned and sank in Discovery Bay, Washington, in 1883, the lower planking is still solid. Wooden parts of ship's tackle were also often of a tougher material. Where hulls have largely disappeared, wooden deadeyes from the sides of sailing ships survive. Blocks may also still be dug from the mud and salvaged.

In the Siuslaw Estuary at Florence, Oregon, a dock once stood where repairs were performed on the lumber schooners that carried northwest timber products to the markets of San Francisco and southern California. Heavy blocks (pulleys) of hardwood with Lignumvitae sheaves (wheels) were occasionally dropped over the side. Jim Alexander was the first to discover the relics at Florence, and to capitalize upon them. Waiting for an extremely low tide, he waded out between the stubs of piling that are the only remaining clues to the former repair dock. Spotting a suspect shape along the edge of the channel, he poked around in the mud to determine whether he had found a relic.

When Jim found a block, the work really began. These blocks are enormous for they were used to raise the entire sail for one mast of a schooner. (The advantage of a schooner over a ship-rigged vessel was that one huge sail was raised per mast instead of three smaller ones, and by pulleys from the deck instead of climbing aloft. Less crew was required.) The larger the sheave, the easier the line turned in the block. It took Jim all morning to dig one of the relics free, and three men to carry it off the tide flat. When telling the story, Jim added, "And there are some bigger ones still out there."

I removed and cleaned one of these blocks and can attest to the effort involved. Removal is hard enough; cleaning is many more hours of work. The Siuslaw River sends a large volume of fresh water through the estuary during the winter storms. Between this and suffocating layers of shifting mud and sand, barnacle growths are periodically killed. Their upright shells break away, but the cemented-down bases remain to become attaching sites of new barnacles. Layer after layer of these bases covered the wooden surface of my rigging block, requiring considerable chipping and scraping before the original surface was reached. Then the sanding of roughened surfaces and bleaching to remove the black from the estuary mud had to be accomplished before the block could be protected by fresh coats of linseed oil.

Metal Fittings

While we were digging in the mud for deadeyes and blocks we were also looking for metal fittings. Iron hardware that lies in the mud is better preserved than similar objects exposed to the water flow. In addition to the things that were discovered in the Siuslaw Estuary, we found iron collars or withes from the tops of masts in Yaquina Bay, Oregon, and iron mast hoops at Butteville on the Willamette River. All of these items from the mud cleaned up reasonably well, though they are fragile from loss of ferrous content.

The Willamette and Columbia rivers around Portland hold several sunken and abandoned hulls, most of which are retired tugs. I have taken a weighted safety line down to some of these and tied it off on one side of a hull. Then, diving companions and I have followed the line down, probed the dark hull with our flashlight beams, and finally followed the line back up to the safety of our dive boat. The line is essential as one can easily drift beneath one of the numerous floating docks or houseboats that line much of the channels—finding the way up blocked about the time the air supply runs out.

In these dark excursions, though, we have removed an assortment of interesting hinges, hooks, and other metalware overlooked by salvors. Most of these are brass, which was commonly used for the door and cabinet hardware in vessels of the 19th and early 20th century.

Copper and brass—which is a copper-zinc alloy—not only resist corrosiveness but deter the effect of marine organisms. Wooden ships were often sheathed with copper plates so the leaching copper salts would kill the shipworms before they could do their damage.

By 1850, shipbuilders were using brass spikes as well as treenails (heavy wooden pegs) to attach planking to the ribs of better-made vessels. As these ships lie in death at the bottom, the copper in the brass continues to leach out, saving the immediately adjoining wood from the borers of the teredo family.

One of my favorite spots to look for these old, square, hand-forged brass spikes is around the remains of the clipper ship, WAR HAWK, in Discovery Bay, Washington. There, by swimming around the row of white-anemone-covered ribs, and scanning the rubble with a metal detector, one can always find a few spikes.

Left: This eye band was originally designed as a two-eye band, but was made as two half circles that bolted together. Right: Hand-forged brass spikes from the *WAR HAWK*, resting in Discovery Bay.

Left: This heavy hardwood block measures 14 by 18 inches across the face. Right: Though one side of the block has come off, the nearly 12-inch-wide iron-bushed Lignum vitae sheave remains.

PART II.
BOTTLE DIVING

CHAPTER 4.

BOTTLES OF THE WATERWAYS

Neither I nor my diving companions initially collected bottles. However, as the sport of scuba diving grew increasingly popular, most of our favorite spearfishing and abalone-gathering locations became crowded and picked over. Relic hunting, on the other hand, could be enjoyed in numerous locations, frequently in places where there were few fish and no scallops or abalone to capture. Bottle and relic collecting greatly broadened the potential for diving locations.

Some later additions to our group were bottle diggers and collectors before they became divers. They had experienced increasing competition for places to dig, and often found the best locations already dug by persons who had not waited to gain permission. I can understand their feelings, for I have tried bottle digging on a few occasions. It is much more relaxed to collect in the water where we have not experienced the problems of property rights and trespass laws.

I have also found that both the collecting and the waterways bottles are different from my bottle-digging experiences. Bottle diving is like gliding along the ocean floor, exploring, and occasionally being rewarded with the sight of an antique bottle cradled in seaweed, or nearly hidden by a drift of sand. The discoveries themselves, though often similar to land-collected glassware, may have the distinct flavor of the sea. A few, like ship's decanters, are specifically designed for use on ships. Others, like the pottery beer bottles that litter many old seaports, are associated with overseas trade. It has not been unusual, while poking

Ships' decanters are one type of glassware prepared specially for the sea. Their wide bases and low centers of gravity helped keep them upright in rolling ships.

Left: The stocky pop bottle (left) carried the product of the Pioneer Soda Works, Portland, Oregon. The Ship's Brand Chutney Sauce bottle (right) bears a likeness of an early steamer. Right: Beneath the layer of barnacles is an interesting old beer bottle.

about in the mud of the bay at places like Port Townsend, Washington, to shake from a lump of mud one of the slope-shouldered white, tan, or tan-and-white clay bottles that carried beer from England. Once they were a low-cost but heavy cargo that could be used in place of ballast in sailing ships, and many of them found their way into the hands of sailors on anchored ships. (Often vessels lay at anchor in port awaiting their turn at the dock.) When the bottles were emptied, they were discarded over the side.

During one dive at Port Townsend, I picked up a pottery beer bottle that was still sealed by most of the cork. Apparently the protruding portion of the cork had broken off, making extraction difficult, so the sailor simply tossed it over the side—there were plenty more below that wouldn't be missed. As I pried out the cork, white foam issued forth, but the beer smelled foul, so I dumped it out. Later, a friend declared, "You fool, all good European lager beer smells that way. If you find any more. . . ." Strange as it may seem, the cold, even temperature at the 70-foot depth had preserved the beer for 80 or 90 years.

Occasionally the clay bottle dug from the mud or sand turns out to be a mineral water container. Although mineral water was evidently not as popular with seafaring men, it was also used as ballast cargo, and some of the pottery bottles found their way over the sides of ships.

Unfortunately for us, sailors did not appear to be as likely as their landlubber counterparts to consume expensive liquor. We draw that conclusion from the large numbers of plain, unembossed whiskey and ale bottles found in the anchorage areas. The docks, particularly where passengers embarked, have been much more productive locations for beautifully embossed glassware. Apparently the officers and passengers fared better than the sailors.

Bottles and Marine Life

Marine bottles have also intrigued me because of their interrelationship with the creatures of the sea. I have come to accept the encrustation of barnacles, or coral in the warmer parts of the sea. Barnacles can be easily removed by an overnight soak in a strong detergent and laundry-bleach solution, but taking them all off robs the glassware of its individuality of the deep. The bottles are more beautiful to me if some of the barnacles, a few of the lacy, thin bryozoan patterns, or reddish coraline algae are left.

Another fascination is the marine creatures that live in bottles: octopi, fish, crabs, clams, and other bivalves. On a recent dive in Gig Harbor, Washington, nearly every bottle picked up was the home of a brightly colored blenny eel. I have often been startled by the fightened exit of such creatures from bottles of other waters.

Octopi are slower to exit, and more unusual to find. Washington's Hood Canal is most apt to produce bottle-dwelling octopi. The soft-bodied creatures readily squeeze into even small-necked containers, at times appearing unable to leave. A side benefit for the collector who is also interested in shells is the shells left in bottles by feeding octopi. The Brinnon area of Hood Canal has given me many small striped Arctic Natica shells; Port Townsend provided a few bottled Boreotrophons.

Some marine creatures actually cannot evacuate their glass houses. Clams often wind up this way, entering in larval form, settling, and flourishing in their secure fortress. In Quathiaski Cove, British Columbia, we found Old Parr whiskey, Holbrook & Co. sauce, and CaLiFig laxative bottles with clamshells inside that were so large either the shells or the bottles would have to be broken to remove them. (This also occurs with freshwater clams. Last year, in the Willamette River, a cruet was collected with a large clam living inside.)

At times, marine life protects as well as adds interest to bottles from the sea. Layers of algae or barnacles shield the fragile glass from tumbling pebbles as flood waters sweep through estuaries —or from abrasiveness of wave-swept sand. Thus, bottles collected from the deep may be in better condition than their land-lubber counterparts.

Collecting Techniques

The characteristics of a bottle, however, may be all but obscured by layers of marine growth. It is obviously impractical to sack up all the encrusted, sand- or silt-filled bottles and try to swim back to the boat or shore with them, but I have devised a few techniques that are helpful. First, a common pot scrubber, preferably the stainless-steel-shaving type, goes along in the goody bag. If the value of a discovered bottle is in doubt, a few swipes at the locations of key characteristics will often help the decision-making. The neck is one place to look. If the bottle was designed for a cork closure it should be studied more closely. When sufficient light is available, the neck can be examined to ascertain whether the find was hand or machine made.

The base of the bottle will also tell approximate age. Certain mold characteristics there show whether the glass was shaped in a machine, and if pontilled, the relative age of blown glass.

Final determination would be with reference to embossing, or lack of it, to be found on the cylinder. Often this can be evaluated by feeling; other times, encrustations must be removed.

The little pot scrubber has served well in most cases, but in Alsea Bay at Waldport, Oregon, we faced a problem it couldn't solve. Barnacle growth such as we had never encountered before covered every bottle. The curse of mariners was so thick on the glass that the growth had become extruded like pipe instead of being conical. The only thing we could do was carefully chip them away from key areas with a diving knife. (Normally this is not recommended because of the danger of chipping the glass.)

At time the creatures of the sea help the bottle-diver in his quest. In Port Townsend, Washington, we found the bottles in the old anchorage area had settled into the mud. A few could be discovered by raking the bits of seaweed that showed here and there. Some clumps turned out to be attached to discarded ballast rocks, but many were on bottles and other relics with just enough of their surface above the mud for algal attachment.

What was most unusual, though, was watching one of the divers head for every large Metridium anemone he saw. He

Left: These barnacled bottles were collected at Port Townsend. Right: Encrustations on a casegin or taper gin bottle from Heriot Bay, British Columbia.

The slope-shouldered black glass bottles were probably used for ale; the larger example (right) is of a style commonly called Hudson's Bay Rum.

seemed intent on harassing the sedentary creatures, which stood a couple of feet tall. Later I asked him what he was doing.

"I was looking for bottles. Those anemones have to find something firm to attach to, and often it is a bottle. I go around reaching under them to feel what they have hold of—and just look at all the bottles I found!"

So far, we have considered only those bottles that are readily visible on the surface of the ocean floor. Beneath this surface are many more waiting to be found. At Heriot Bay, British Columbia, we started with the glassware that could be seen. Before long, though, we began to find more by reaching into the mud, and as one was drawn out another would be felt beneath it. It wasn't long before we found ourselves working down to elbow depth, finding older bottles the deeper we went.

In that location, I tried several forms of rake, thinking that the most ingenious would be a slender-tined pitchfork with the tines bent. Unfortunately, each kind of rake, including the specially adapted pitchfork, hung up on more pieces of wood than bottles. In that location searching by hand was the only feasible method.

The pitchfork was later tried at a location in the Willamette River. This time, instead of raking the deeper mud, we used the fork as a probe. In that manner it was a success; we found an old Chinese pottery jar the first time it was used.

Some bottle divers have gone farther. Dredges have been put to use, but there are mixed feelings about them. At Port Townsend I interviewed the operator of a small, one-man dredge with the idea of using the material in my "Bottle Digger" column in *Treasure* magazine. I received plentiful information (even a couple of nice bottles) but was told, "Please don't use my name in the column; I don't want the ecologists on my neck."

I share his concern—not from what the ecologists might say, but what indiscriminate dredging might do to the environment. Where he was using the dredge, the area had already been dug to shallower depths by underwater diggers, and carried little living marine life, anyway. If the dredging had been in a rich

These two bottles from Quathiaski Cove, British Columbia, have been homes for resident clams. Such is a fairly common occurrence in other places as well.

This unusual milkglass whiskey bottle was found during a dive in the lower Willamette River below Portland. It dates from the 1890s.

clam bed, or even a place that hosted the tiny creatures which are the beginning of the food chain, it would have been a different story.

For the time being, at least, I shall be content with taking the glassware and other relics where the environment will not suffer as a result.

CHAPTER 5.

ESTIMATING A BOTTLE'S AGE

Two of the most frequently asked questions (other than, "Where did you get that?") are, "How old is it?" and "What kind of bottle is it?" Having passed the inquirer off with, "I found it out there at the 80-foot depth" (that normally suffices for non-divers), one is then faced with the more difficult questions. Let's tackle the age first.

A knowledge of bottle-manufacturing techniques and when they were used is one of the best methods of finding the age answer. Occasionally, a bottle will bear the embossing of a company that was in existence for only a short time, and that really pins it down. Such is the case of the Cottle Post & Company soda-pop bottle. That company was in business in Portland, Oregon, only from 1879 to 1881. It is obvious from library research that any Cottle Post & Company bottle is circa 1880. However, out in the water or on the beach there is no opportunity for reference work, so the following are some general factors that can be used for rough estimates.

There are several elements in the manufacture of glassware that can help in estimating age. These are the kind of material used, the type of mold employed in the case of mold-blown bottles, the method of holding the product while finishing, and the effects of patents and legal acts. Even so, we must limit the application of these factors to American and some European glass, for handmade bottles are still being made in places like Mexico.

Glass Color

One of the quickest but one of the roughest indicators of age is the color of the glass. Color is the result of ingredients, which

41

differed with the passage of time. From the earliest glass manufacturing in this country until 1850 or 1860 (depending on the manufacturer) common bottles were very dark, a color usually referred to as "black glass." It is extremely dark, like obsidian or natural glass, and has about as many varied impurities.

Better quality glass, and nearly all that followed 1860 in common glass, contained sand and alkalies such as soda for the basic ingredients. These components result in a clear, greenish product. Impurities continued to be present, however—like iron in the sand—which colored the batch anything from a pale green to a dark, smoky olive green. Often, through the 1870s, the darker coloration is found in common wine and ale bottles.

Most bottles for such things as patent medicines continued to have a green or blue tint, although by the 1890s such coloration was losing favor. The fact that such tinting could be removed by adding manganese to the batch had been known since 1810. Although this technique was quickly picked up for finer glassware, it did not become prevalent in bottles until consumer demand (partly attributed to home preserving of foods in glass jars) brought it about around 1890. It is the manganese in the glass that reacts to ultraviolet in the sun's rays to produce purple or amethyst glass.

Although purple coloration is one method of detecting manganese glass, bottles in the water do not turn purple because the required ultraviolet rays do not penetrate the water to sufficient depth. (If the bottle diver has a yen for "desert glass," the appropriate finds can be placed on the patio roof during the summer.) Occasionally one is found, though, that turned purple before it was discarded into the water.

Manganese continued to be utilized until around 1917. Some authorities attribute its decline to World War I which cut off the manganese supply to this country. At that time, selenium became the decoloring agent, and continued to be used by some companies until about 1930. Selenium also reacts with ultraviolet, producing an amber color.

The preceding color factors were unintentional. Some colors, however, are intentionally added to the glass. The vivid dark-blue color so sought by collectors was produced by adding cobalt to the batch. The Cumberland Glass Mfg. Company of Bridgeton, N.J., was well known for its cobalt-blue bottles during the 1890s; other firms, like Maryland Glass, later took over the cobalt trade.

Through various decades, greens were induced into the glass with copper or chromium, reds with selenium or gold, browns with nickel and carbon. The most expensive to produce was ruby red, which required gold at the rate of one ounce for about 50 to 60 pounds of glass. Gold-produced reds are seldom found in bottles other than fine decanters.

By 1900 the use of milkglass, made by adding zinc or tin to the batch, had come into vogue. It did not really attain acceptance in the beverage industry, but has been used extensively by cosmetics manufacturers and to some degree by cheesemakers.

Occasionally, as a bottle dries out, it surprises its finder by developing various forms of rainbow shades. This is not a color combination imparted into the glass, but a refraction of reflected light by glass particles separating from the bottle. In other words, this is decomposition of the glass, and the bottle is shedding loose particles. In time, tiny flakes will usually appear, and if the decomposition is inside the container as well, will collect as a semi-transparent residue in the bottom.

Heavier decomposition results in glass with a frosty appearance, or even sanded-appearing glass. At times the frosty coat will appear in swirled patterns. This is due to content variations in mixing (the batch wasn't mixed thoroughly) and the effect of blowing the paraison or bubble of glass into the mold. If the deterioration is not too severe, it can be removed by buffing with a clean buffing wheel and very fine grit. The interior of such bottles can be cleaned with diluted hydrofluoric acid.

The existence of deterioration of the glass is not an indicator of age. In some areas, the minerals of the soil and water combine to form acids which etch glass. In addition, some glass compounds resist decomposition more than others.

Generally speaking, the diver or digger should take steps to protect any bottle that appears to be old enough to be free-blown, is of black glass, and is worthy of such efforts. Such old bottles may begin flaking away as soon as the outer surface dries. On one dive in the northern end of Puget Sound, a companion discovered an old, probably free-blown, brandy flask. Despite encouragement to keep it damp, he allowed it to dry, and I helplessly watched as the outer surface flaked away. It could have been preserved by keeping it wet until it was treated. Treatment would have consisted of soaking in a 0.2% solution of sulfuric acid for four or five days, then coating the bottle with acrylic or polyester resin.

Pre-1900 bottles often have impurities in the glass. At times bits of broken glass can be seen embedded in the sides, as such broken pieces were not only put back into use, but were thought to make the batch melt smoothly. These and other impurities are often referred to as "seeds" by collectors.

One form of seed considered desirable is bubbling. In the smaller batches of old glass factories, the scum (called gall) was moving to the surface much of the time. As it did, it developed bubbles, which, in turn, were picked up in the gather to be blown into glassware. Since the blowing was usually down into a mold, most bubbles moved toward the neck. As the glass stretched out there, the bubbles became elongated; when finishing occurred, many became twisted at unusual angles.

With the advent of the bottle machines and large factories with huge batches and quality controls, most bubbles disappeared.

Glass Molding

A second help in determining if a bottle is old enough to warrant bringing up from the depths is the type of mold it was blown in. Again, molds are only an aid, another indicator, for some glass factories continued using styles of molds long beyond their competitors. In the extreme, I have seen Mexican glass molded in recent years with techniques utilized in America in the 1830s.

Most 18th century common glass containers were free blown (without molds). During the early decades of the 19th century, free-blown bottles continued in heavy use for wines. Better bottles of the late 18th century and early 19th century were usually pattern molded (started in a pattern, then blown larger outside the mold). Not all free-blown bottles are round and bubble-like. Some were squared or six-sided by paddling; others were made cylindrical by rolling. Naturally, they lacked seams imparted by molds, but other techniques could erase seams, so a bottle should not be labeled as free-blown without other factors confirming its age. (To further confuse the issue, there have been a few specialty wine decanters free-blown in this century.)

Turnmolded bottles are often mistaken for free-blown. This is understandable, for it was fashionable, particularly in the 1890s, to twist the forming bottle in the mold to erase the seams. The resultant product was smooth, like a well-made free-blown bottle—if the mold was not rough. However, molds of the time had irregularities which imparted indistinct circular lines in the glass as the bottle was turned. All the experienced collector has to do is hold the suspect bottle up to the light to see these faint marks.

The earliest true molds were the dip molds, consisting of a hole bored into a block. The gaffer (glass blower) simply blew the paraison in the dip mold long enough to shape the cylinder. It was then extracted, and the neck, shoulder, and lip were formed by hand. Most of my dip-molded examples are ale and wine bottles from the older ports of British Columbia. These are of dark, smoky glass, but not as dark as true black glass. From first glance, they are difficult to tell from turnmolded, for the molds were bored, and boring is apt to leave circular irregularities in the mold.

Distinctions, though, are present: dip molds were tapered for bottle removal (they had to be slid up and out) while turnmolds were hinged and straight-sided. Dip molds ended short of the shoulder (occasionally leaving a line where the paraison slopped over), while turnmolds normally went full length, making a product that shows no hand working except near the lip.

Two-piece molds, hinged at the bottom, are thought to have been first used around 1810, overlapping the time of the dip molds and continued to be used as late as 1880. At first, like dip molds, they formed only the cylinder, and are called open molds. Later versions were closed molds that also formed the shoulder and neck of the bottle. Most two-piece-molded bottles I have found have been 12-faceted and small, the size that could be used as medicine or perfume bottles.

As mold technology moved to the 1870s, the old dip mold had a couple more pieces added, to become a three-piece mold. The lower part of the bottle thus formed had the same taper, but the neck and shoulder were more symmetrical, having been formed in a mold. Now a seam was clearly visible around the top of the dip portion, and another seam extended down each side of the neck and shoulder, combining on opposite sides into inverted Ts.

The lower part of a three-piece-molded bottle still had to be slipped upward. However, the shoulder and neck portions of the mold swung away, so they would not erase a raised design. Three-piece-molded bottles are among the earliest with raised letters, although the embossing is limited to the shoulder.

Leaf molds superseded three-piece molds in most glass factories by the late 1880s. In these molds, the dip section was omitted and two hinged sides extended the length of the container to be made. Earlier leaf molds tended to be of the post type, meaning the two leaves that formed the sides joined around a post at the base. Bottles thus shaped have a circular pattern within the base.

The post was easier to center the mold parts around. But, by the 1890s, molds were improved to where the post was not

This free-blown demijohn shows the irregular shape common in such glassware. Note the slight angle of the neck.
(Don Bergseng photo)

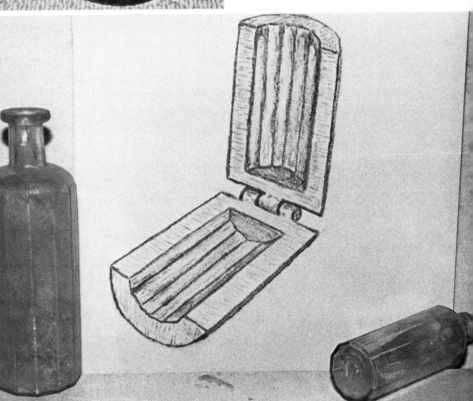

An artist's sketch illustrates the style of two-piece mold that formed these bottles. A rough pontil mark obscures the base seam of the bottle on the right.

needed for centering, and the cup-bottom leaf mold evolved. Its products are distinguished by the base seam being around, instead of in, the bottom of the bottle. About this time, also, molds were developed that included the lip of the bottle as well as the neck, and the art of embossing was fully developed. Molds like this would move on into the machine age.

Before moving on to the machine molds, there are two specialty molds of the pre-machine era that warrant mention. One of these is the plate mold. It is a mold with a space to accept lettered plates that would result in different embossing on otherwise identical bottles. Either kind of leaf mold could be adapted as a plate mold by cutting away for plate insertion. The numerous embossed drugstore bottles of the 1880s and 1890s were made in such molds, as well as many bottles of the smaller patent medicine companies.

The other specialty is more complicated. It is the blow-back mold, commonly used to produce fruit jars, but also used to make other large-mouth containers like battery jars and anchor-light lenses. In Nehalem Bay, Oregon, we found both battery jars and cylidrical anchor-light lenses that appeared to have been made in blow-back molds.

This class of mold, in use since the 1850s, forms the lip of the jar or full length of the cylinder of other products. Above the cutaway of the jar was a ring in the mold where the glass was blown outward and thus thinned. At this point the molded glass could easily be broken, and the thin edge ground down.

In my early days of bottle and relic diving I was inclined to leave on the bottom anything that had a screw top, fruit jars included. What made me stop and learn a little about them was that one day after a dive, as I was visiting Lynn Blumenstein in Salem, and browsing through one of his books while we talked, I noticed a picture of a fruit jar like one I had left in Yaquina Bay. It was worth $16. I have since learned that, with blow-back molds, screw-top jars can be old and valuable.

These dip-molded bottles probably date from the 1870s, although the technique is much older. They are not pontilled, nor are they dark enough to be black glass. The line where the dip mold ended at the shoulder is faintly visible; necks are irregular.

These turnmolded bottles appear smooth and seamless. However, the telltale lines from mold irregularities, impressed as the bottles were spun, are present. They are more distinct in the example to the right.

The smooth pontil technique still left [a] mark, as shown on the base of this wi[ne] bottle, but there were no sharp edges [to] cut or scratch. Black residue frequen[tly] left by the red-hot iron pontil gave t[his] the additional name of graphite pon[til.]

A bottle blown in a three-piece mold stands beside a sketch of the type of mold required to form it. Faintly visible are the seam around the top of the dip section and the seams that run down opposite sides of the neck and shoulder to join it.

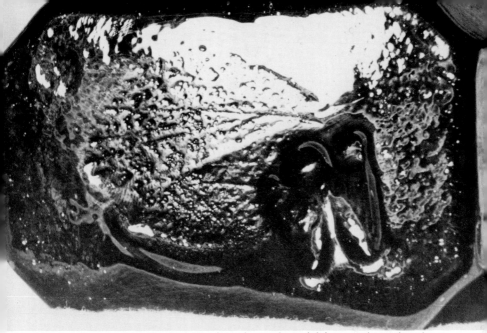

One of the more popular methods of remedying the roughness left by a rough pontil mark was to reheat or fire-polish the base of the bottle. That method was used on this snuff jar. The "W" is an impressed maker's mark, probably Whitney Bros.

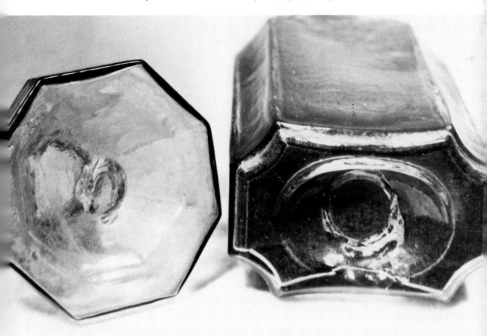

These bottles found at the portage point above Willamette Falls were held by the rough pontil method. There is sufficient broken glass along the edge of the pontil mark to cut one's finger. Both the ink bottle (left) and the spice bottle (right) were blown in molds.

Pontil marks were occasionally ground and polished from better quality items. A chip occurred as the pontil was being ground from this art-glass vase. Note the wearing along the edges.

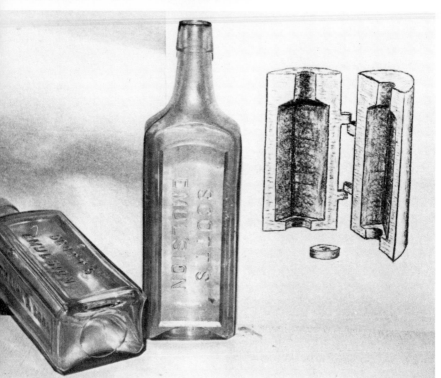

The invention of the leaf mold permitted rectangular molds as well as other shapes. These bottles were blown in a post-bottom leaf mold, something like the sketch in the background.

Laid-on rings of the decades of glass-blowing from 1860 to 1890 frequently show defect lines that travel around the top of the neck. This example is more obvious than most applied lips.

Cup-bottom leaf molds evolved in the 1890s and became more sophisticated with revision. Later ones included the lip of the bottle in molding.

Tooled tops of the 1890s and 1900s are occasionally identifiable by seams running partially up the neck, as on this bottle. Often, though, the seams are wiped away by tooling, leaving only the absence of defects as clues the lips were not applied.

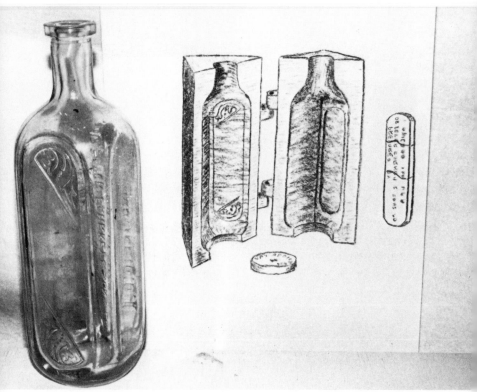

One variation of the leaf mold was the plate mold. In the side of one leaf was a recess to hold any of a group of interchangeable engraved plates. Individually embossed bottles could thus be blown in the same mold. This particular bottle was blown in a mold with a cracked plate, as shown in the accompanying sketch.

An emblem of the sea from the days of sailing ships was used as the maker's mark of the Capstan Glass Company. This example, showing the wound and trailing line, appears on the base of a glass tumbler.

Another emblem of the sea, the anchor, has been used by several glass companies. This one, superimposed on an H, was the mark of Anchor Hocking Glass from 1938 until 1946.

The imprint of the snapcase fingers is clearly visible in the lower part of the back panel of this bottle. The snap was intended to grasp around the base of the bottle and leave no marks, but occasionally the gaffer's assistant would become too eager and take the bottle before the glass had cooled to firmness.

Blowback systems have been in use since the 1850s, probably incorporated into a variety of types of molds. Their products are recognizable by the ground (and sometimes polished) lips. This early threaded bottle has been ground and polished; the light lens only ground.

Molds used in machine blowing are similar to the later leaf molds but include mold parts to form the total lip. Generally, such molds leave a seam around the base of the lip, and another onto and across the top of the lip. Exceptions to this occur when bottles have been heat polished to smooth the seams. This was done primarily on beverage bottles, like milk containers, before molds were refined to have only a very slight seam mark.

Many early machine molds left a circular, seam-like mark on the bottom, referred to as an "Owens ring," after the early bottle-blowing machines invented by Michael J. Owens, around 1903. Such rings, which slop over onto the sides of narrow, flattened bottles like whiskey flasks, were made by the device which cut off the flow of glass to the mold. Other early machines, used until the 1930s, failed to line up the side and neck seams.

A bottle should not be discarded simply because it was machine-made. Many have value, particularly the whisky and pop bottles.

Pontilling

A third indicator of a bottle's age is the method by which it was handled for finishing, and applies only to pre-machine bottles. After a bottle had been blown, it had to be removed from the blowpipe and held while the neck was finished. Until around 1850, this was accomplished by gathering a gob of molten glass either on a blowpipe, or an iron bar called a pontil, and using it like glue to attach the pontil or pipe to the bottle. When the finishing process was complete, the bottle was broken away. Unless the base was reheated (called refiring) to melt the rough edges, or they were ground off, there remained a rough-edged scar, commonly called a rough pontil mark.

Around 1850, someone discovered that a pontil, simply heated until it was red hot, would stick to a bottle without the usual bit of molten glass. The use of the bare iron pontil still left its mark, but it was smooth. Since iron heated to this degree forms black slag, bits of this material occasionally adhered to the bottle; it looks like graphite. Thus, the smooth pontil mark is sometimes referred to as a graphite pontil.

In many glass factories the use of the smooth pontil was short-lived. About the same time the smooth pontil technique was discovered, another person invented a metal-fingered, forked rod with cups that gripped the hot bottle. This device was called a snapcase, perhaps for the way it gripped the glassware. It gained in popularity, replacing both types of pontils by 1870. Unlike the pontils, it left no mark unless someone miscalculated the readiness of the bottle and placed the case on while the glass was too soft. Occasionally, bottles of the 1860 through 1890 decades show the imprint of the snapcase in their sides.

At times, one comes up with another mark on the base which doesn't fit any of the above. This is the sand pontil mark, one which I have found only in black glass bottles with a kickup, or raised portion of the base. The kickup was used in bottles intended for beverages like wines that left sediment in the beverage. The indentation in the bottom was intended to cause the sediment to lie in a ring, which prevented sliding on a flat bottom when the bottle was tilted for pouring; it helped prevent clouding of the drink. (The kickup has continued through the years in many wine and champagne bottles.)

Apparently the use of an oversized pontil formed the kickup while holding the bottle for finishing. It is believed these pontils were dipped in sand to facilitate their removal, for the texture of such marks is frequently rough and sandy to the touch. They lack, however, the broken edges of the rough pontil mark.

Lip Finishing

The final item that I use for dating, which is based on the method of manufacture, is the manner in which the lips were finished. For instance, most of the earlier bottles that did not carry a large volume simply had their necks cut from the blow-pipe and the end flared out to receive corks.

Special implements for affixing lips to bottles have been known since around 1850, but were not in general practice at that time. Only glassware that carried large volumes, like wine demijohns, had additional glass laid around the lip as reinforcement. By 1870, however, it had become customary to wrap some molten glass around the sheared lip and shape it to form reinforced lips on most bottles. These early laid-on lips were rough, with fusing often incomplete enough for the sheared or broken neck to show through, and roughness like wood grain remaining where the extra glass was stretched around the top.

By the 1880s, lips were smoother, with better fusing of lips to necks, but still showing minute fracture-like lines. During this time it was common to see drips below the neck, that were flattened by the lip-shaping tool. A popular feature, particularly on beverage bottles, was a sloping, slender ring below the lip. This second ring is often referred to as a drip ring.

As the 1890s arrived, the shaping of lips had been pretty much refined so that flattened drips and irregularities were unusual. Rounded tops became popular—very much so in the turnmolded wine bottles. Combination tops of patent medicines and smooth, flat-sided whiskey-cork closure styles continued through the decade and into the appearance of early machine molds of the 20th century. Inside threads, introduced in the 1870s, became popular in whiskey bottles.

By the turn of the century most closed molds included the formation of the lip. Bottles from these molds required no laid-on rings and were simply "tooled" in finishing. Tooled bottles can be detected by the seams which proceed part way up the lip.

Special Features

There are a few special features about the necks and lips of pop bottles that not only make them enjoyable to collect, but help in their dating. For instance, the ring and marble closure was invented in 1860. Though it was never very popular in this country, one may find a foreign bottle in some old seaport. The metal and rubber disc with a wire loop came into being in 1872, followed by the wire bail and porcelain stopper in 1875. These were all stoppers that remained with the bottle. The marble and the disc stoppers stayed inside the bottle and interfered with cleaning, so that they were eventually declared unsanitary. The wire bail and porcelain system, however, stayed around to compete (for a while) with the familiar metal crown cap, which was invented in 1892.

A percentage of old bottles found by the collector will also have a marking, normally on the base, which will aid in narrowing the estimate of time of manufacture. This is the maker's mark, a letter or symbol engraved into the base of the mold. Obviously, makers' marks are not to be found on free-blown bottles. Earlier mold-blown, and more common glassware, seldom have such marks; newer and more elaborate examples are most apt to be marked. A reference to such books as *Bottle Makers and Their Marks*, by Julian Harrison Toulouse, may help in dating the find.

As an example, glassware with a nautical capstan wound with heavy line was the mark of Capstan Glass Company, Connellsville, Pennsylvania. It was operated by a corporation that also owned Anchor Cap Company, and made principally tumblers and jars. The capstan mark was used from the time the plant opened in 1918 until it was absorbed as Anchor Hocking Glass Corporation in 1937.

Plain anchor marks were used by the Anchor Glass Company, London, England, around the turn of the century, and in recent years, by Glashuttenwerke Ibbenbüren of Ibbenbüren, West Germany. The anchor superimposed on an H was a mark of the Anchor Hocking Glass Corporation—the successor of Capstan— with which most of us are familiar, since it has grown to become one of the largest glass producers in this country. The anchor and H were used, often with the words "Anchor Hocking," from 1938 until 1946, when the anchor was discontinued in favor of the mark, "Anchorglass."

There is obviously some overlap in the use of makers' marks. Often, continued use of a maker's mark leaves the researcher with information that narrows the dating only to a twenty- or thirty-year span, during which a number of changes could have taken place that affect the value of an individual bottle.

If one feels a bit confused after considering all these factors, it is understandable. I was confused when I first learned them— and many times afterwards as I attempted to apply the information. I was most misled by dark, smoky-colored bottles until I realized just how black true black glass is; also by various plunger marks and mold defects that look something like pontil scars. With practice, though, I have learned to make field estimates and select which glassware to carry back to the boat.

Let's take some examples that show the application of factors of glass technology in making these field evaluations. In the illustration of the hinge-bottom, two-piece mold on page 00, two 12-faceted bottles are shown. We know this particular type of mold was in use from around 1810 to 1880. This gives us the outside parameters for our estimates. The smaller one, lying on its side, shows a rough pontil mark. Since rough pontils were generally superseded by 1860, declining in use from about 1850, we now have it narrowed down to a 50-year period. There is no helpful maker's mark, but the glass, rather clear despite some decomposition, suggests a fairly late period in our time estimate, since it is a common bottle, not a decorative piece. We could now say our little bottle is circa 1850.

The larger, upright bottle in the illustration, though similar in appearance and blown in the same kind of mold, has some differences. It was held with a snapcase (no pontil mark). The mold was still an open type (no seams on the shoulder or neck), and the glass is similar in clarity, so it is a bit newer, perhaps circa 1860.

If these were bottles with patented stoppers we could further narrow the dating by patent dates. Incidentally, there are a few more items related to patents and laws that are helpful. The words "Trade Mark" may go back as far as 1870, but the practice of embossing the fluid-ounce capacity on bottles did not become common until 1910.

When Prohibition was lifted, the requirement was added that all liquor bottles for contents beyond certain proof must have embossed on them "Federal Law Forbids Sale or Re-use of This Bottle." This occurred in 1936 and applied to imported as well as domestic liquor.

Now that we have covered a few ways to estimate the age of bottles, let's go on to that other important question, "What was the bottle used for?" The answer is important, for knowledge about the previous use of a bit of glassware increases its value to the owner. I also have some prejudices—some favorite bottle types.

CHAPTER 6.

FAVORITE BOTTLE TYPES

Beers

We were diving in Nehalem Bay, Oregon, seeking to expand our knowledge of a shipwreck we had found, when we discovered a relic hole. Numerous malt-extract bottles were gathered; then from the mud appeared a long, slope-shouldered bottle with a knobby top. Embossed vertically up one side, in large block letters were the words, "ENTERPRISE BREWING CO., S.F. CAL." A thrill came over the dive, for here was our first circa-1880 beverage bottle from the area, and beverage bottles are among the most desired and most valuable to be found.

This was obviously a beer bottle. There has been a tendency by some collectors to look upon beers as representative of the "common man's drink," but perhaps because of the more classless society of this generation, beer bottles are rising in popularity. Certainly we were very pleased to discover this one.

Beer bottles are probably the most abundant form of glassware along the bottoms of our waterways. Both sailors and travelers must have consumed large amounts. Yet, the older ones are interesting, often nicely embossed, and not very common. Actually, before the method of pasteurizing beer was developed, it continued to work and build pressure that would explode a bottle. Similarly-shaped bottles of the early 1870s usually olive green instead of beer-bottle brown, were ale bottles.

Our earliest beer bottles were rather crude, sometimes lacking the polished finish we expect of most glassware, and they had rather heavy, roughly applied blobby tops. Even then, the traditional beer-bottle brown color was apparent. Although many, probably small, breweries continued to use these cheap bottles, others, like the Enterprise Brewing Company, purchased better grade bottles, nicely embossed, and usually capped with a porcelain and wire bale arrangement (lightning stopper). These are most sought after by the evolving group of specialized collectors of beer bottles.

In the 1880s, corked beer bottles with the flared-out second ring, or drip ring, were also in use. These are better finished than the old blob-top cheap bottles, and occasionally embossed. Embossing of beer bottles, however, really reached its peak about the time of the invention of the familiar metal crown cap in 1892. Many nicely embossed crown-cap beer bottles, both hand finished and machine made, are extant and are sought after by collectors. An interesting practice during this time was for the brewery to retain ownership of the bottles. Embossing often included "NOT TO BE SOLD" or "PROPERTY OF . . ." as well as the name of the brewery.

Seaports have their own special beer bottles awaiting the diver. These are the pottery bottles that arrived from Europe in ballast, and came to litter the floor of former anchorages and dock areas. Hoodsport, Washington, once contained many such bottles, though now most of these have been gathered. Port Townsend, Washington, still yields a few, as do many other Puget Sound ports.

While collecting the various types of pottery bottles, I have been interested in the potter's mark that came to be stamped into one side of the bottle, just as the glass manufacturer frequently had his emblem imprinted in the glass or carved in the mold.

The Enterprise Brewing Company bottle plucked from Nehalem Bay, Oregon, appears on the right. The smaller companion originated with another San Francisco brewery. Unfortunately the wire bales have rusted away and the porcelain stoppers lost.

It could be said that these are the sea's own beer bottles, for they are found most abundantly on the floor of the ports through which they were brought to this country. The older of this group, on the left, lacks a maker's mark, but the others are stamped J. MACINTYRE & Co., LIVERPOOL; MURRAY & Co., GLASGOW; and MIDLAND POTTERY, MELLING.

The late 1890s and 1900s were years of vogue for embossed beer bottles. These examples were found in the harbors of Quadra Island, British Columbia. Those in center and right of the picture are brown rather than typical amber-brown.

Precursors of our beer bottles, these four likely contained ale. The two to the left were blown in three-piece molds. Older ale bottles were made of black glass; these are a smoky green.

Two-quart and gallon demijohns were often used for whiskey. The clear two-quart one brought up from the Willamette River floor by the author was undoubtedly covered with wicker which has rotted away. (Karen Combs photo)

The crudest of these beer bottles, left, was found at the old dock area of Yaquina City, Oregon, which was at its peak in the late 1870s. It shows no maker's mark. The next two, probably blown in San Francisco and marked R & Co., were likely manufactured in the early 1880s. The late 1880s examples to the right were both made by the D.O. Cunningham Glass Company. All are sometimes called export beer bottles. Huge barnacle bases remain on the bottle second from left.

The 1920s brought a time of fat beer bottles with rings around their necks, as shown on the barnacled two-quart from Nehalem, and the quart and pre-stubby from Yaquina City, Oregon. Notice the bulbous area below the lip. Particularly on the larger beer bottles, this was often used to hold the wire of a lightning stopper.

Interest can be restored to plain bottles with the addition of authentic labels. The center bottle is an 1890s turnmolded example in red glass; both end ones are clear, though they have begun to turn purple. The dark object in the example to the right is the cork, which survived many years of immersion. (Labels courtesy of Bergseng's Coins & Collectibles, Portland, Oregon)

A few of the later beer bottles warrant some attention. Our present twist-tops and stubbies did not suddenly appear. As the machine age arrived, following Owen's invention in 1903, the beer bottle continued to have a long neck. Later the body of the beer bottle tended to thicken, but the neck was still long, something like the malt-extract bottles of preceding decades. During the 1920s, these "fat" numbers were commonly seen, a few still made with a groove below the lip so either the crown cap or wired-on lightning stopper could be used. Style, at this time, also dictated one or two rings around the neck.

It was these long-necked bottles that the loggers from Seabeck, Washington, drank from during their ferry rides back from the Olympic Peninsula and a hard day's work. Impatient and thirsty, and lacking a "churchkey" opener, they simply broke off the top of the bottle on the ferry rail. As we found large numbers of bottles with broken-off tops beneath the former ferry slip near Brinnon on the Olympic Peninsula, we wondered how many cut lips had been suffered by thirsty lumberjacks.

Not all beer bottles were amber-brown. Anheuser-Busch bottles were traditionally clear with a bluish tint; several others were bottle-glass green until the 1920s. A few breweries continue to use clear glass.

Whiskeys

Although we were happy to find the Enterprise Brewing Co. bottle at Nehalem, we were even happier as a strap-sided Van Schuyvers whiskey bottle was probed out of the silt. Whiskey bottles, according to many collectors and dealers, are the most sought-after type of bottle. There is little doubt that they have about as varied forms and embossing as any glass container. It is said that some of the first embossing went into the original Booz bottles around 1860.

Perhaps I am a little more appreciative of embossed whiskeys since the first one that I owned was given to me by Irv Erickson, a fellow bottle-diver—and promptly smashed as another diving buddy dropped a weight belt on it. It was many dives later that I obtained another embossed whiskey. Perhaps it was the elaborate embossing of the gift Jesse Moore & Co. whiskey that hooked me, or maybe it was the embossed antler design, or the glistening amber color. At any rate, I have found whiskey bottles among those most appreciated in the goody bag.

The discovery of whiskey bottles seems to vary with location. Most of the smaller flasks that I have picked up came from ferry landings and work areas. Apparently, travelers carried small pocket flasks, either pint or half-pint "picnic" bottles, and discarded them when empty. Larger sizes have often been found in anchorage areas, but more frequently about docks where saloons once stood, and in places where garbage was formerly dumped.

Earlier whiskey bottles tended to be dark in color, the so-called black glass. This coloration continued, particularly in Scotch and other imports, into the 1880s. A typical bottle of this kind was squatty, blown in a three-piece mold, and often included a drip ring beneath the lip.

By the 1880s, whiskey bottles were regularly being made in ambers, reds, and other colors. An occasional example has more than one color—a result of adding glass to the batch without proper mixing, or when the lip was laid on from a different batch. It is the color and the embossing which make these bottles desirable. Their relative scarcity makes the prices soar. Many whiskey bottles have values in the hundreds, a few even in the thousands.

Whiskey bottles were also made in various shapes—cylindrical, round, rectangular, figural, and the classical log cabin. A few had handles added; many of the larger ones originally were covered with wicker. The woven reed material does not survive in the water; basketry and reed handles disappear, but the shapes are distinctive enough to recognize without their covers.

The old crockery whiskey jugs could well be added to the list, but these are rarely found intact under water. They were normally saved and re-used for various purposes. At Butteville,

These bottles recovered from Nehalem Bay are embossed, "W.J. Van Schuyver & Co., Portland, Oregon." They date from the 1890s. Many Van Schuyver bottles had inside-thread closures; these do not.

Fluted shoulders were popular in the 1890s and 1900s. The older of these two, the embossed Oregon Importing Co. bottle on the right, is a very dark amber. Smaller embossing reads, "We Neither Rectify nor Compound." The later paper-label example on the left is of lighter amber glass, and could have been used by Oregon Importing Co., Portland, or Roth & Company, San Francisco.

This Jesse Moore embossed whiskey bottle was given to the author by Irv Erickson of Everett, Washington. The first one was broken by a dropped weight belt; this is the second one. Irv has found many embossed whiskey bottles in Washington waterways. (*Treasure* Magazine photo)

This group of 19th century whiskey flasks was contributed by former travelers of our waterways. The flasks are (left to right): pumpkinseed from Nehalem, coffin flask from Portland, union oval from Port Gamble, and strap-sided picnic out of Nehalem Bay. The union oval is the oldest of these styles, strap-sided the newest.

Oregon, we found a number of whiskey jugs where a steamer had blown up, but all were broken in the explosion. I have found only one clay American whiskey jug intact under water.

In the 1880s and 1890s, when the cylindrical, long-necked shape was prevalent in quart-size whiskeys, several shapes of smaller-sized bottles were popular. One was the union oval, which had rounded shoulders and downward-tapering body. A cross section of the body would be somewhat oval, more boat-shaped.

Another favorite was the pumpkinseed, which was thinner and rounded on all four corners. Since it was thin (glass as well as the bottle), a large percentage of this style are found broken. At Nehalem we found embossed but broken bottles of this kind.

Another flask that shared popularity with the union oval and pumpkinseed was the coffin flask. It had rounded shoulders like the union oval, but front and back were flat, and the edges peaked like a roof. The flat panels, peaked edges, and tapering body gave the bottle an appearance not unlike the old pine box.

While the lips of union oval and pumpkinseed flasks were rolled, the coffin had elongated, flat-sided cork closures, a shape that could be readily incorporated into molds. It thus continued into the era of tooled rather than laid-on lips.

By 1900, the little picnic flasks were disappearing from the market and being replaced by several forms of pint flasks. The strap-sided flasks were still being manufactured in picnics as well as pints, but most of the newer bottles intended for pocket use were eagle pints. They were characterized by straight sides, rounded shoulders, and slightly rounded lower corners. The lips were flat-sided with small drip rings. Most were made for paper labels; the majority were machine-produced.

Even so, eagle flasks have some value. The older ones, if of clear glass, contain manganese and will turn purple or amethyst if left exposed to the direct rays of the sun. Later examples, like those embossed with a spider-web pattern, contained selenium as a clearing agent, and turn amber or straw colored in the sun.

Only a few months of exposure to summer sun will create color if the necessary ingredients are present.

By 1920, screw caps had become standardized, and most whiskey pints and fifths used that type of closure. The magic words that destroy value in whiskey bottles are "Federal Law Forbids Sale or Re-use of This Bottle." It is embossing that was required by law when Prohibition ended in 1936, and only recently was repealed.

Wines, Champagnes, and Brandies

We were relatively new to bottle diving when we began finding relics at Yaquina City, Oregon. One of the first treasures of the dive was an 1890s turnmolded wine bottle with an interesting green tint. A short time later, my diving companion, Dick McGarvey, found one similar in shape and size, but of brownish glass. By the end of the day, a dark, almost black, brandy bottle had also been found. We have been spending our diving time looking for relics ever since.

It is true that wine bottles and their relatives are among the most plentiful of older bottles, but they also tend to be rather crude, have free-flowing lines, and are usually of colorful glass. Even after 1860 some wine bottles continued to be free blown and tended to be short, globular, and irregular. It was later that the traditional styles of bottles evolved that distinguish the type of wine contained. Generally, by the 1880s a tall bottle with sloping neck and no distinct shoulder indicated a dry wine, while sweet wines tended to be bottled in cylindrical bottles with rounded shoulders. Red wines were usually bottled in glassware of darker color.

Many wine bottles of the 1880s were blown in three-piece molds, though leaf molds were already common. Closures were often a simple laid-on ring placed slightly below the actual lip. (This design is copied in many machine-made wine bottles of today.) Others had longer, flattened closures with a drip ring beneath, like some of the beer and whiskey bottles of the time,

Before the 1870s, wine was bottled in black glass containers like those on the left. However, ale and other beverage vendors used similar glassware. By the 1880s, sweet wine was found in nearly clear bottles, which, except for indented bases, were practically the same as those in use for some Scotch whiskeys.

Most of the 19th century flask designs were discontinued as the 20th century dawned. The eagle flask became the most common type, with three variations shown above. On the far left is a hand-finished version; the spiderweb-embossed and dark amber examples in the center were machine made, the amber one most recently. It was made about the same time as the rectangular pint (right), just before Prohibition.

Turnmolding was popular through the 1890s. Even the group of wine bottles on the left, with simple laid-on bands, has been turnmolded. An interesting smoky black, darker near the base, they probably held red wines. Other turnmolded wine bottles shown have smooth, symmetrical, globular tops. The bottle from Yaquina City is the large one in the center.

Champagne bottles are found in several sizes, but their shape has stayed relatively the same for a hundred years. The larger bottle on the left, with swirled irregularities in the glass, was free-blown. Center example lay in the mud of Rock Bay, British Columbia, where its lead seal was preserved.

but can be distinguished from the latter by the kick-ups or indented bases. It was in the 1890s that turnmolded wine bottles, like those we found at Yaquina City, became popular. During that decade, symmetrically globular lips were also fashionable.

Wines have since been bottled in a wide variety of containers. Even the more common ones occur in differing sizes and colors of glass. Champagnes, on the other hand, have been sold in glass that has not substantially changed in the last century. At least there is no mistaking a champagne bottle. Our experience is that champagne bottles tend to be found in groups. Perhaps no one drank a single bottle of champagne on shipboard; champagne was the symbol of the party. In Heriot Bay, British Columbia, for instance, I hovered over one spot and picked up a dozen champagne bottles that had lain there for about 80 years.

Other Liquor Bottles

In a way I feel I am slighting some friends by lumping the rest of the spirits bottles together, for as I look over the shelf on which they sit I realize that individually each has brought a thrill of discovery. Such bottles usually come singly, however, and occupy much less space in the collection.

My favorite of the other spirits bottles is the casegin or taper gin. It is dark in color, black glass in the older ones and smoky green in those from the 1870s and 1880s. Like the pottery beer bottles, the taper gins have a connection with the sea, for their design provides for convenient packing in cases for shipment. Thus they have character in color, distinctive shape, and frequently an encrusted mark of the sea upon them.

Unfortunately, most taper gins are thin-walled, and like the little pumpkinseed whiskeys, are often found broken. I well remember the frustration of Heriot Bay, British Columbia, which must have a record number of broken taper gins. I would see a square black form protruding from the mud, but on pulling it up would find only part of a bottle. Rock Bay had its share, too, and for several years it seemed as though I never would find a complete one. Even now, I have only one.

Although gin was discovered in Holland in the middle of the 17th century, and most taper gin bottles are from that country, gin was also very popular in England. English gin bottles, usually of more recent vintage and either clear or bottle-glass green, are plentiful in our waterways.

When the English crown placed a tax on gin in 1750, bitters were added to the spirits and it was sold tax-free as "medicinal bitters." Today, bitters bottles are classified as either liquor or patent medicine. In North America, bitters were usually sold as patent medicines, among the most famous of which are Dr. Hostetter's Stomach Bitters and Lash's Kidney and Liver Bitters.

Bitters bottles are found in many different shapes, but most frequently have a square base, rectangular sides (not tapered like the casegin), and a dark amber color. Unlike the gins, bitters found here are usually American products. Perhaps because of the popularity of the patent medicines in this country, locally produced bitters flooded the market.

Schnapps is another liquor that came in rectangular bottles and arrived from Europe in ship's cargo. Like many bitters bottles, its containers had short necks and cork closures. Typically, it was of a unique dark-green glass, lighter than the also-Dutch casegins.

Kimmel bottles from Germany are occasionally found in our waterways. They, too, are short-necked and squared for packing, but are recognizable by their dark amber color and flattened corners.

The subject of liquor bottles found in the Pacific Northwest should not be left without mention of the Hudson's Bay rum. Since the 1820s, the Bay has played an important role in Pacific Northwest matters. Its early western headquarters were at Fort Vancouver on the Columbia River in the edge of present-day Vancouver, Washington. It operated a number of fur-trading posts in what became the Oregon Territory, Washington Territory, and finally those states, until 1860 when the Hudson's Bay Company pulled its remaining operation north of the Canadian border.

This taper gin was found in Rock Bay, British Columbia. Though it shows the typical crudeness of shoulder and neck formation, it lacks a pontil scar, and was probably made in the 1870s.

Many styles of bottles have been used for brandy. The crescent brandy bottle (left), so named because of the raised crescent that held the wax seal, is circa 1870. The squatty bottle (right) is of emerald-green glass, and once held Portuguese brandy. It appears to have been made in the 1890s. The curved flask in the center, with an embossed fire-breathing dragon, held brandy from Cognac, France, and is circa 1900.

Bitters was an outgrowth of English gin, but most bitters bottles in this country originated here as patent medicine containers. The Hostetter's Stomach Bitters, a product of Pennsylvania, was found at Yaquina City. Lash's, from San Francisco and other locations, was encountered at Nehalem.

Gordon's English gin bottles have retained the same style through the decades. The bottle on the left is bottle-glass green with a laid-on lip characteristic of the 1880s. Center example, tipped to show the snarling boar's head embossed on the base, is of clear glass and was made with an early bottle machine. These two, from the Willamette River, had cork sleeve and glass stopper closures. Later pint (right) has a cork closure and was found at Whaletown, British Columbia.

Udolpho Wolfe's schnapps bottles were not tapered, but they did follow the case-gin pattern in rounded shoulders, short necks, and flat-edged cork closures. The dark green tint of the glass is unique. These were found at Portland, Oregon.

Despite lack of embossing, these are some of my favorite bottles. They are (left to right) French liqueur bottle of cobalt blue glass, German kimmel, and Hudson's Bay rum.

These bottles are commonly called Hutches by collectors (short for Hutchinson stopper, the type of closure used). The Portland Soda Works bottle to the right has an embossed eagle, as does the Cottle & Post bottle shown below. Cottle & Post, in business from 1879 to 1881, eventually sold to Northrup & Sturgis, Portland Soda Works.

Bottles of this type are often referred to as blob-top sodas. The bottles on the left and in the center were found in Tillamook Bay, Oregon. Although the bottle to the right is similar in appearance, it is later, as evidenced by the porcelain stopper and embossing on the base that shows it was made by Streator Bottle & Glass, which did not start operations until 1881.

What is little known is that Hudson's Bay Company started a number of subsidiary enterprises, including distilling. Several kinds of distilled spirits were produced at Fort Vancouver and marketed in Husdon's Bay bottles. Most bottles were unembossed, but of a distinctive style of black glass which collectors have come to call "Hudson's Bay Rum."

Pop Bottles

Brent Forsberg suggested that we dive Hobsonville Point in Oregon's Tillamook Bay. It had been the site of a flourishing sawmill with its satellite community during the 1880s. Nothing remains of the buildings; only a few weathered stubs of piling, some brick, and concrete foundations show that industry once occupied the spot.

As we slipped beneath the waters of the bay we passed over waterlogged slabs cut from the outer surfaces of logs, circles of teredo-riddled piling stubs, and occasional building bricks. Rusted hulks of machinery protruded from the sand and silt near the piling farthest from shore. There we found the bottles —mine a dark green blob-top bottle with an eagle embossed on the side; Brent's a green-tinted, embossed bottle of similar size.

This time pop bottles provided the excitement of the dive. Brent had picked up a Hoffman & Joseph, Albany, Oregon, pop bottle; mine was a Cottle, Post & Co., Portland, Oregon, bottle. Both were from around 1880, fairly valuable finds.

The location of these items was typical of pop-bottle discoveries in the waterways. Seemingly, sailors of ships in the anchorages left beer, whiskey, and other hard liquor bottles, but around docks and ferry landings, where families gathered for travel or just to spend a Sunday afternoon fishing, one is more apt to encounter pop bottles.

Such bottles could be divided into two distinct groups—import bottles and domestic containers. What Brent and I had found were early domestic soda-pop bottles, squatty in shape, with sloping shoulders, and necks topped with blobby lips.

These blob-top sodas were the popular style until wired-on corks were supplanted by the Hutchinson stopper.

The pop bottle that I picked up at Hobsonville was from a company, Cottle & Post, which was in business in Portland only from 1879 to 1881. Within a few years the business was Portland Soda Works (Northrup & Sturgis), which still maintained an eagle embossed on the bottles but used primarily the Hutchinson-type bottles. These are recognizable by their straight cylinders and extremely short necks. Their lips are also blobby, though most collectors reserve the title of blob-top soda for the pre-Hutchinson bottles. The Hutchinson, named for the inventor of its rubber-and-metal stopper, was very popular, so is the most frequently found pop bottle with a blob top. The stopper would identify the type, but it is usually rusted away.

Looking much like the Hutchinson-stoppered bottle is the gravity-stoppered soda. Without the stoppers, they are difficult to tell apart, for both were sealed internally, the Hutchinson by a metal and rubber disc attached to a wire, the gravity by a glass oval with a rubber ring. Another that divers should be aware of is the Codd-stoppered bottle, which was closed by a glass marble that rolled in a specially shaped neck. These bottles were not very popular in America, except with children who broke the bottles to get the marbles, but they are often seen on English bottles. Thus, they are more often encountered in a port area.

The other group of soda-pop bottles is the import type. It is true that some imported pop bottles looked very much like those produced in North America, but there is a fascinating difference. During the time of cork closure, there was a problem of corks drying out during the long voyage by sea and the pressures of the contents "popping" out the shrinking, drying cork. To keep the corks damp, the contents had to be kept against the closure. As this was not possible with an upright bottle, the import bottles of the day were made with round bottoms— they couldn't be stored upright.

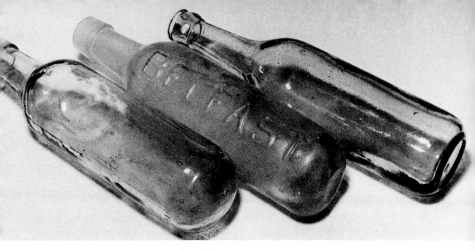

Import pop bottles of the 1870s and 1880s customarily had round bottoms to prevent their being left upright, allowing the corks to dry out and shrink. Center bottle is embossed Ross's, Belfast. Far example is a transition bottle, with a top suitable for a crown cap, wired-on stopper, or cork. From the mid-1890s, it retains much of the rounded type of base.

The 1890s and first two decades of this century saw an abundant variety of interestingly embossed crown-cap pops. This group from Puget Sound and adjoining waters of Canada are (left to right): Seattle Bottler's Association, Pacific & Puget Sound, Whistle, and Eagle Bottling Works. Only the Eagle is hand tooled; the others are machine made.

Ross's Belfast bottles are perhaps the most commonly found of the imported round-bottomed group. There were, however, many others, and many unembossed rounded-base bottles. At the time the crown cap was appearing, import bottles were designed with lips that would accommodate crown caps, had large enough rings to hold wires for lightning stoppers, or could be closed with a cork. Interestingly, these import bottles differed a little in basic shape, though the round base was modified with a flat portion so they could be stood upright. Their makers weren't going to rush into this newfangled style.

The invention of the crown cap, and its acceptance around 1892, drastically affected the soda bottling industry. Crown-cap bottles, substantially cheaper to use, quickly replaced all other closures. This was still an era, however, of small, community bottling works, and a continuing need for individualized containers. In fact, with the invention of the bottle machine in 1903, individually embossed bottles became even less expensive. The time of the early crown-cap bottle became one of the richest in available variety of embossed soda-pop bottles.

We have been particularly impressed with the crown-cap pop bottles of the Puget Sound area. One of my favorites is a Pacific & Puget Sound, Seattle, bottle with an eagle embossed on the shoulder. There are many embossed eagles, but this one is carrying a bottle slung beneath its beak.

Mineral Water

Out from the ferry landing at Port Townsend, where the water had reached a depth of perhaps 60 feet, a brown object lay partially protruding. As I reached under it and pulled, a reddish-brown pottery jug emerged. Tall, straight, and unglazed, it has a design and some lettering stamped into the clay. The top line of the marking read, *"Leonhardiquelle,"* letters around the emblem, *"Selzer Wasser."* This was a mineral-water container, one of many to be found in our waterways.

It may seem strange that water was transported over the seas, but during the latter part of the 19th century both domestic and

Pictured at left are the author's favorite pop bottles, Thorpe & Co. Red Hand Brand. They are heavy glass, green bottles made by Cannington & Shaw, St. Helens, England. The closure is another style intended to get around the problems of shrinking and popping-out corks, inside threads in the neck and a wooden bolt. One normally has to look in northern Puget Sound or British Columbia waters to find them. The one on the left was discovered at Rock Bay, British Columbia; the medium-sized was in Heriot Bay, British Columbia; the smaller one, which is complete with wooden bolt, was a gift from Pete Craddock.

English mineral water and utility bottles of the latter part of the 19th century are of green glass, usually blown in three-piece molds, and have simple laid-on lips. Among them, however, are examples of particular interest to nautical collectors, for the Johnson mineral-water bottles from Liverpool carried an embossed likeness of the card of the mariner's compass.

foreign mineral waters were sought as beneficial to the health. The pottery jug from Hessen (German state) which was found at Port Townsend was only one of many types imported to this country. There were several, from different foreign areas, that arrived in similar pottery containers, unglazed, with a simple rounded top, and clay handle.

Mineral water also arrived in this country in glass bottles. One of the most popular came in a cylindrical, dark green bottle with a short neck and globular top. The bases of such bottles are embossed *Hunyadi Janos Saxlehners Bitterquelle.* Contained in them was the Huyadi Janos mineral water, bottled by Andreas Saxlehner, Budapest, Hungary.

English mineral water also came to this country in green bottles, though these were usually unembossed, slope-shouldered, and quite plain. A few have a compass card embossed on the shoulder; many have maker's marks on the bases showing manufacture at St. Helens, England. Identification cannot be positive in the case of the English bottles, for the same containers were sold for use with other products besides mineral water. About all that is certain is that they were a cheap, common bottle of the 1880s and 1890s and mineral water containers was one of their uses.

The English mineral-water bottles are not the only ones in this category. Some that are commonly referred to as ales, brandy, wine, or pop bottles, particularly if unembossed, may have been used for other purposes. The individual bottle that you are holding may have had a number of purposes. When bottles required craftsman skill and considerable labor, it was the usual practice for merchants to stock a small selection for various small businesses to use, and bottles were re-used for different products. Harold Lucas, a collector in Bend, Oregon, showed me an embossed Asparagus Bitters Company bottle with a Bythinia Santa Barbara Mineral Water Company label over the embossing. What kind of bottle is it? The embossing says bitters; the label and contents claim mineral water.

European mineral water arrived in North America in pottery as well as glass. The dark green bottle to the left contained Hungarian mineral water and is embossed on the base, Hunyadi Janos Saxlehners Bitterquelle. Reddish brown pottery jug contained German Selzer Wasser.

Domestic mineral water was marketed in a wide variety of glass containers. The Buffalo Lithia Water (left) two-quart container is embossed with a very ugly representation of a maiden pouring water from a pitcher. The small I-adore-a Natural Mineral Water bottle is of early 20th century manufacture.

The elaborately embossed quart cathedral pickle jars so often found inland are seldom seen in the waterways. Plain cathedral jars like these on the left and right seem to replace them. The larger jar was found in Tillamook Bay, Oregon, and is of clear glass which has begun to turn purple now that it is exposed to sunlight. The smaller unembossed jar, from Puget Sound, has similar characteristics. Center bottle, from Quathiaski Cove, British Columbia, is of later manufacture (probably 1920) and is turning amber from the sun and selenium content of the glass.

These impressive pickle bottles of the 1890s stand nearly a foot tall. They are of glass that contains a substantial amount of manganese. Two summers on the patio roof have given them enough sun to change their color from clear to a rich amethyst.

Bottles from the Galleys and Kitchens

It may appear from the preceding pages that all our seamen did was drink while in the ports. A few conversations with current sailors would tend to confirm this, but we know it is not so. In our waterways we also find the containers from which food had been taken for the table. The greatest abundance have been recovered from former dock areas, leading to the thought that garbage from nearby households ended up there as well.

In only a few cases can the source of foodstuff containers be pinpointed. One location was in Quathiaski Cove, British Columbia, at a spot Pete Craddock, a local friend, suggested we dive. "Up there on the bluff," he said, "was one of the old homesteads of this area. I think they probably brought their garbage down the hill and threw it over."

Pete was right. Below the bluff we found marmalade crocks, snuff containers, pickle jars, patent medicine bottles, dishes—all that one might expect from an old homestead. Some of the glassware was broken by hitting the edge of the rock cliff, but most was beautiful after the accumulation of sea life was removed.

One of the favorite groups of household and galley bottles is the pickle and preserve bottles. They are impressive in size, often holding a quart or more, and distinctive in shape. Although embossed lettering is unusual, various designs in the body and neck are common. Their use also goes back sufficiently far to find an occasional pontilled example, and many have bubbles and other irregularities from their hand-shaped creation. During the early part of the 19th century, preserve bottles were often made with elaborate, arched, cathedral-tower-like sides. Such early examples were made of shades of bottle-glass green. Later cathedral pickle bottles lacked the elaborate design, and were normally of clear glass.

Around 1900, style dictated that these bottles be made in an oval or semi-oval (one side flattened) cross-sectional design. Still, they continued to be large, tall, and end in wide-mouth, though tubular necks. Into the machine age this neck style continued, retaining a simple rolled lip, and often a second decorative ring around the base of the neck. With the machine age came the waxed-paper disc closures, so the pickle and preserve bottles of the early part of the 20th century normally had an inset in the lip for the paper cap. During this time, embossing, particularly on the base, became common. A few even have patent dates included in the embossing, which help to give a rough estimate of age.

In fur-trading days, ships frequently crossed to the Orient to dispose of their furs and to take on a cargo of spices and extracts for sale in New England. Spices and extracts were bottled and sent out from Boston and other Yankee ports, a tradition that has remained. A few of the older, and many of the newer extract and spice bottles are to be found in ports today. Shape and color vary, but one thing is common—they are small. The *J. W. Hunnewell, Boston* bottle is as typical as any, and more interesting from one standpoint. It stands over 6 inches high and has a neck with an opening 5/8" wide, but the sides are so concave and thickened they come within 3/8 inch of meeting on the interior of the bottle. (Where were the consumer protection agencies in those days?)

While spice and flavoring bottles could be characterized as small, the sauces could be described as slender. The older sauce bottles, the peppersauces, were elaborately decorated and uniquely designed. Some of the bottles of the first part of the 19th century shared the cathedral design with the relish and pickle jars, but were mere spires by comparison. Others were of slender beehive pattern, or had slender fluting. Most were of bottle-glass green, a coloring that continued through changes of sauce and style.

Perhaps the most abundant of the sauce bottles is the Lea & Perrins Worcestershire Sauce. Or, maybe it only seems that way, for their bottles remained unchanged significantly, even when they changed suppliers in 1877, for around 50 years. Their slim, sharply-shouldered, long-necked bottles have been found in waterways all over the Northwest. Most are embossed

Lea & Perrins vertically up the side of the cylinder, with Worcestershire Sauce around the shoulder. Closure was a cork sleeve through which a glass stopper slid. Others followed suit: Holbrook & Co. with a similar bottle, others at least following the slender shape.

One deviation in the form of sauce bottle is the chutney. Perhaps this is partly due to its East Indian origin, but the chutney sauce bottle has a shape of its own, larger, wider-mouthed (almost like a pickle bottle), and heavier. It seems to carry the atmosphere of the sea, particularly the "Original Ship's Brand Chutney" with its embossed early steamer.

While most sauce bottles are slender, the olives are actually skinny. In fact, I wouldn't doubt that the olive-oil bottles inspired Popeye's cartoon companion. The olive-oil bottles have the most slender necks of any of the bottles I am aware of. Typically, olive-oil bottles have a slightly flared base, slender body, and long, skinny neck, with a simply reinforced lip. Olive bottles are also slender, but are a straight tube with slightly flared lip, looking somewhat like an old seacaptain's telescope.

One distinction that I have found in comparing galley bottles with household bottles is relative size. Crews were larger than the normal-sized family, so bulk purchasing was appropriate. As a result, larger food bottles are often found in the waterways.

One example of this occurred as we were diving the old steamer port at Corvallis, Oregon. I had run into an area of river bottom that was fairly covered with freshwater clams, and I was having trouble spotting the old bottles beneath them. Then a long glass neck protruded distinctly above the mass of shells. I thought I had discovered a quart whiskey bottle, one with interesting vertical embossing. On reaching the sunlight of the surface, however, the embossed words were found to read, "Columbia Brand Salad Oil, Union Meat Co." The Union Meat Company was a Portland, Oregon, firm which, in the 1890s, advertised a specialty of ships' supplies. In 1919 its name was changed to Swift & Co.

Large food bottles have also been discovered in older Puget Sound ports, and in the steamer points of call of the British Columbia coast.

Earlier, I used to bypass many of the galley bottles, particularly things like catsups because they were screw-cap bottles. Then I learned that catsups came in the same traditional shape as current ones, and with screw caps, before the bottle machine was invented. Every time I left an embossed early catsup on the ocean floor I had left a dollar behind. Now I pay more attention and have discovered a nice group of galley types, including a cut-glass piece of a castor set, some interesting milk-glass cheese jars, and some marmalade crocks.

Even the fruit jars were sacked up or left behind, depending on mood and availability of other things. Perhaps it was the rough old green English fruit jars made by Cannington & Shaw and Kilner Brothers Glass that changed this. In their heavy glass of shades of green, occasionally square shape, and roughly applied lips, tapered on the inside for glass stoppers, they were irresistible. With increasing knowledge of other jars came the desire to bring home many through the years. After Alex Kerr told me that the Kerr jars had originated in my home city of Portland, Oregon, I developed a new interest in the Kerr Economy and its successors.

Nor had I realized that our present fruit jars, yes the screw tops, started way back in the 1850s. The older ones are recognizable by the high shoulder and the lips that were ground to smooth the place where they were broken away at the constriction of the blow-back mold.

Different types of closures add interest to fruit jars. Besides the old porcelain-lined zinc screw tops, there is a wide variety of glass lids. Some of these, particularly the more modern, were tightened down by rings resembling the outer part of a screw top, but many were held tightly in place by wire bales, levers, or bridges with a set screw. However, the waters don't treat these metal parts too kindly, and the bottle diver unfamiliar with jars may find himself confronted with an interesting guessing game.

Chutney sauce, brought by the British to the world market from India, was shipped in several styles of glassware. Most were unembossed, as is the example on the left. Such plain bottles were not exclusively chutney bottles; other contents might have been brandied cherries or pickles. Embossed Ship Brand Chutney bottle on the right is rare. Both bottles were made by Cannington & Shaw, St. Helens, England.

The first encounter with a barnacle-covered shape, like the bottle in the center, brought to mind a telescope. It is, however, an olive bottle. To the left are two olive oil bottles in the typical skinny form. A Dodson & Hils food bottle (right center) and barrel mustard (right) complete this group. The barrel mustard contains a large amount of manganese in the glass and has turned purple.

Port areas occasionally yield large galley containers. This Columbia Brand Salad Oil bottle was on the floor of a Willamette River port; the Shirriff's and Braid's Best were in the old steamer dock areas in the islands of British Columbia. Smaller bottle holds about 12 ounces, the larger nearly a quart.

In this group of early 20th century preserve jars, the one at the far left, made in a hand-plunger machine, seems to follow some of the aspects of the cathedral jars. The plain jar and the 8-faceted J.H. Heintz bottle in the center have some amethyst coloring. A Pearly Monia (bivalve) grew inside the Empress jar, second from the right. A 1931 embossed patent date and lip encrustation of coralline algae grace the example on the far right.

Around the turn of the century (1900) the use of milkglass had risen in popularity. These containers, found at Whaletown, British Columbia, were used for Mac-Laren's Imperial Cream Cheese, as evidenced by the embossed lettering, keys, and cows' heads on their bases. (Smaller one to the right is missing its lid.)

Peppersauce bottles of the 1880s might be fluted or beehive, like the two on the left. Holbrook & Company design seems to copy the Lea & Perrins even to the glass stopper. Lea & Perrins example shown was made by the pre-1877 supplier. Plain bottle, second to right, probably contained a hot sauce; on the far right is a circa 1910 Garton's HP Sauce.

Cut-glass castor set bottle, found at Port Townsend, Washington, adds a unique note to the collection. Grinding and chipping at the top was to fit a metal top which has rusted away.

Marmalade containers of the past century were often pottery. The plain example on the right, like the other two, bears the pottery company stamping in the base, "Maling, Newcastle."

This 1890s milk bottle, with its misshapen neck and applied lip, seems strange, but the embossing has clear-enough meaning. (*Western & Eastern Treasures* Magazine photo)

Catsup bottles have changed little since these were made around 1890.

Markings on the bases of these obviously later English jars show they were made after Kilner Brothers became incorporated in 1873. The glass is still bottle-glass green, but the manufacture is much more sophisticated.

These English fruit jars in green glass lack distinguishable makers' marks, but the techniques suggest they were made in the 1870s, possibly earlier. The jar in the center was blown in a mold with a cracked base plate. All were found in Heriot Bay, British Columbia.

The shoulders of early Mason jars are separated from the zinc screw caps only by the red rubber gaskets. Style dates back to Mason's patent of 1858. The jar on the right was blown in a mold and ground to finish the top. The machine-made Ball jar is probably circa 1905, although Ball used semi-automatic machines as early as 1898. Both are bottle-glass green.

A number of early fruit jars used glass lids and wire bales. The Lightning (left) shows a patent date of Apr. 25, 1882 on the accompanying lid, but this hand-finished jar was made by Putnam Glass Works which went out of business in 1871. The similar-appearing Atlas in the center, also of green glass, was machine made. Later Atlas (right) is of clear glass and has the holder for the bale molded into the jar.

In addition to screw-top jars, the Ball company manufactured wire bale and glass lid versions that resembled Atlas jars. Example on the left, showing a patent date of July 14, 1908, is green. The pint and half-pint models are clear.

Kerr Economy jars made their appearance in Portland, Oregon, in 1903. The center jar, with only "Economy" embossed on the cylinder, is one of the original Kerr products, as evidenced by "Portland, Ore." embossed on the base. The 2-quart (left) and pint have the later locations of Sand Springs, Oklahoma, and of Chicago embossed on the bases.

The Hazel Atlas Glass Company of Wheeling, West Virginia, manufactured these Strong Shoulder Mason jars prior to World War I, as evidenced by the purple tinting they are acquiring.

An assortment of Canadian fruit jars is to be found in the northern waters. Queen was the trademark of Smalley, Kivlan, & Onthank, a Boston, Massachusetts merchandising firm, but this jar (left) is marked, "Made in Canada." Crown and Perfect Seal are true Canadian products in every sense, the former manufactured by Diamond Glass, Montreal, which later became Dominion Glass, producer of the Perfect Seal.

At Nehalem, Oregon, we came upon a hoard of fruit jars, and a scattering of different types of glass lids. The evening puzzle became figuring out, from pictures, which lid went on which kind of fruit jar. We never did get them all matched up; on the basement shelf is an assortment of unidentified glass lids.

A few clues on fruit jars: if it is blue or green it is normally older and worth more. If the top edge is ground, or at least the bottom has a rough Owens ring, it is old enough to bring back, but if the base is textured (a current practice), forget it.

Patent Medicine Bottles

Men of the sea are usually thought of as being healthy, or of suffering silently through the evils of scurvy and various sea scourges. They are represented as hale and healthy, or dying in sudden plagues. It would seem that the plagues and scurvy took tolls away from our waterways of the Pacific Northwest, for comparatively few medicine bottles are encountered in comparison to the beer, whiskey, ale, or even food containers. Their abundance is not nearly what can be found by bottle diggers poking around where great grandfather once had his privy. The floor of the sea does have its scattering of medicinal bottles, however, enough to add interest and an occasional laugh to the bottle dive.

One of the interesting types of medicines to be found is the sarsaparilla. Many people of this generation think of "sarsparilla" along with soft drinks. It is true that American Sarsaparilla is one of the ingredients of root beer, but this is a different plant. The true sarsaparilla is a Central American vine that the mariners of old Spain took home with them in the 1550s as a sure cure for syphilis. It wasn't.

In later times, sarsaparilla was replaced with mercurials as syphilis cure, and finally mercurials were abandoned in favor of antibiotics. Meanwhle, beginning in this country around 1850, sarsaparilla was said to have value as a blood purifier, and fortunes were made on it. At its height of popularity in the 1880s and 1890s, it sold for what a skilled craftsman, like a shipwright, would call a long day's wages for one bottle. People like James C. Ayers and Charles I. Hood were still telling the public that sarsaparilla, particularly their brands, were good for scrofula, king's evil, debility, malaria, boils and syphilitic affections —or whatever else might be bothering you.

Perhaps men of the sea suffered from more of the above than other maladies, for I have found more kinds of sarsaparilla bottles in our waterways than any other type of patent medicine. Not only have the popular Hood's and Ayer's sarsaparillas been found, but lesser-known brands like Dr. Henry's and Dr. Murphy's have also turned up in the ports.

About the time of the Civil War another kind of cure-all made its appearance in large numbers. That was the celery and cola compound. Presumably it was the cocaine in the cola that gave the sufferer a soothed feeling, but it also gave the sarsaparilla pushers a lot of competition along our shores. In Nehalem Bay, we found an abundance of these bottles, most of them from the Celro-Cola Company in Portland, Oregon's major seaport.

Even while we cannot attribute much use of patent medicines to the seafaring folk, they certainly brought many bottles with them in their cargoes. The invoices of Hedden's Store in Scottsburg, Oregon, once the seaport of the Oregon Territory gold rush, show numerous shipments arriving by the coastal schooners LILY, LUCY, and BEULAH. Hedden's was a general store, but no license was needed to sell patent medicines, nor even such things as tannic acid to disinfect wounds or laudanum to dull the pain. Large shipments of such merchandise arrived at small ports all along our coastline during the 19th century, and were dispensed to the ailing and injured by local merchants. In the case of Scottsburg, the nearest medical doctor was twenty miles away by boat—the only means of travel.

Some old-timers feel that, in the absence of trained medical practitioners, these early patent medicines saved lives. Certainly most of them had some medicinal herbs with diuretic and other qualities, though their application was close to guess-work.

Since most ships lacked trained medical practitioners, the same was probably true on the waterways as well as on shore. We can only speculate, now, at the relative value of the old proprietary medications.

We have been inclined to draw some conclusions from the kinds of proprietary medicines we have found in our waterways. There is, as earlier mentioned, quite a number of sarsaparilla bottles to be found, but also a scattering of other remedies. In Canada we came across the only consumptive cure bottles, but perhaps this was by chance. It seems no fluke, though, that we found literally dozens of malt extract bottles in Nehalem Bay, Oregon, and a fair scattering of this product in other nearby harbors. Yaquina City and Waldport had their share, but someone in Nehalem was really a large user. Why there was this reliance on malt along the Oregon coast we cannot explain.

There has been a general scattering of products like Scott's Emulsion, which, with its codfish oil, was beneficial to the health and also reflects a closeness with the sea. Another frequent medicine was the liniments. It is fairly obvious that it was hard physical labor raising and lowering sails, scrubbing decks, weighing the anchor, and—the way it was done in the old days —unloading and loading of ships. Photographs show the stern of many a lumber schooner thrust against the dock, with timbers being carried up gangplanks and thrust into the holds. Aching shoulders and backs must have been commonplace.

Beneath these port areas we found Hoff's Liniment, Minard's Liniment, Hamlin's Wizard Oil (which claimed to cure diphtheria and toothache as well as rheumatism and lame back), H.H.H. Liniment (which was originally a horse medicine), and many others. It should be noted that another horse medicine, Spavin Cure, was advertised as being for "man or beast." Liniments in the 19th century were intended for either human or animal use, whatever the market might be. Some were also recommended for either internal or external use. They had enough alcohol so that if you preferred to skip the rubdown, you could just drink the contents and feel no pain.

Our two most abundant sarsaparillas, and likely the most frequently found patent medicine bottles of our waterways, are Hood's Sarsaparilla (left) and Ayer's (right). Ayer's was the first, starting around 1857, with Hood's gaining rapidly in the 1880s. (*Western & Eastern Treasures* Magazine photo)

Many brands of sarsaparilla are to be found, as nearly every medicine company of the 19th century sold its own brand. Dr. Murphy's was bottled at the Coos Bay, Oregon, drug store of Henry Sengstacken (authentic label added). Dr. Henry's Sarsaparilla attracted a crab which grew too large to be shaken out of the bottle.

During the 19th century, multiple patent medicine products of the same company were the rule. Log Cabin Sarsaparilla was sold by the H.H. Warner Company, famous for their "Safe Cures." (The Warner Company had originally been in the safe business. When they found patent medicines more profitable, they used their safe on many of their bottles.)

Following the Civil War, celery and cola compounds became popular. Paine's Celery Compound (left) is a Vermont product of the 1880s, though it was still popular at the turn of the century. Celro-Kola (center and right) was a Portland, Oregon, proprietary medicine.

Dr. D. Jayne's products were only a few of those to arrive in western seaports. By the 1880s, ships' holds contained many cases of patent medicines in their cargoes. (*Western & Eastern Treasures Magazine* photo)

THE DISCOVERY OF AMERICA.

Although the implications of this advertising card seem a bit ridiculous, the sarsaparilla plant was in use in America when Columbus arrived. Sarsaparilla did not cure syphilis, though, as the Spaniards had hoped.

Scott's Emulsion, a cod-liver oil product, was first marketed in 1876, and is still in use. Earlier, bottle-glass green, embossed bottles are of the general shape of the example on the left. Side embossing reads, "Cod Liver Oil" and "With Lime & Soda." The man-and-fish embossing, shown on the right, began being used in the 1890s; this example is a Canadian-made bottle from the 1920s.

Advertising cards (often called trade cards) for Scott's Emulsion carried a basic theme that tied it with the sea. The little "Sailor Boy" (left) was used on many of their cards. The man with the codfish (right) eventually became the Scott's emblem embossed on their bottles.

Dr. Kilmer's Swamp Root Kidney, Liver & Bladder Cure bottles occur in varying sizes. The smallest is a sample bottle. The author was puzzled by the embossed design on the larger bottle until he found out it wasn't an apple but a kidney.

H. H. H. (left) started out as horse medicine in Stockton, California, in 1868, later became the Celebrated HHH Liniment & Medicine. After the originator moved to Philadelphia in 1880, an eastern version appeared (center). Both contained large amounts of alcohol. (The Stockton version contained 65%, or was 130 proof.) King of Pain (right) was another California product, originating in San Francisco in 1869. It is relatively scarce.

Hoff's and Minard's Liniments are from early this century, and are for external use only. Mexican Mustang Liniment originated in the 1850s, but this bottle dates from the 1890s.

Medicine bottles with a flavor of the North—these held Canadian products. Bickle's Anti-consumptive Syrup bottle (left) is bottle-glass green. The later, machine-made Dr. S.N. Thomas Eclectic Oil bottle (center) is clear, carries embossing stating the contents were for internal or external use. Norway Pine Syrup (right) was a product of Wood's, Toronto, Ontario. This bottle, too, was machine made.

These three patent medicine containers are of fairly recent vintage (circa 1920). Creomulsion bottles (left), Fritola (center), and Mayr's (right) are collectable, but of little value as yet.

Dr. King's was introduced in 1868 as a Consumption remedy, but became a cold remedy in the 1890s when the term of "Consumption" lost popularity.

Laxatives must have been important to the people of our waterways, judging from the variety and numbers of bottles to be found. Both Dr. Pitcher's and Dr. Fletcher's Castoria (right) and California Fig Syrups (center) were among the most popular. Bottle on the far left, Sterling Products Ltd., was found in Quathiaski Cove, British Columbia.

Malt extracts appear to have been popular along the Oregon coast. The 1870s bottle (left) was found at Yaquina City; Cla-Wood (next left) at Waldport; and Schusters (second from right) was abundant at Nehalem. Jno. Wyeth (right) is from Portland.

Such aches and pains from the labors of the sea we can understand. Sailing ships conjure up pictures of muscular men rushing to the rigging, flexing their muscles at the capstan, or standing spraddle-legged, barefoot to the knees, holystoning the deck. What we haven't been able to explain is all of those laxative bottles that are down on the ocean floor. Syrup-of-fig bottles have turned up the length of our Northwest coast, to say nothing of both Dr. Pitcher's and Dr. Fletcher's Castoria, plus a few others.

When the Food and Drug Act was passed in the United States in 1906, labeling requirements caused the decline of many of the popular patent medicines. The unfavorable publicity that led to the passage of the act probably was as much influence. In Canada, the Proprietary or Patent Medicine Act was passed, with similar consumer protection intent. Patent medicines are still with us, but they are not as strange, as much fun to find.

Medicine Chest and Pharmacy Bottles

While we joked about the Tonic Vermifuge, Swamp Root, King of Pain (for a monster hangover), and other patent medicines, we were also finding evidences of serious medical treatment. From places that once were beneath anchored ships, we lifted from the mud items like bandage jars from the ship's surgeon's chest, and bottles from the ethical dispensing of pharmacies ashore.

Medicine bottles from the older ports were plain, and most that we recovered were blown in two-piece or three-piece molds. It is not unusual for them to be twelve-faceted, that is, with twelve narrow panels comprising their cylinders. Ship surgeons and pioneer druggists were inclined to order their pill- and liquid-medicine bottles through salesmen of the glass companies like Whitall Tatum. By the 1890s, wholesale drug firms included an array of prescription or pharmaceutical ware in their catalogs. Both drugs and glassware could then be ordered from the same supplier.

With the invention of the plate mold, most larger drugstores obtained their own individualized containers. While the bottles were standard catalog items, the embossing was unique through the plate inserted into the mold. As we dived the dark, muddy Willamette River, we tired of the struggles with diving lights that unexpectedly went out, but were, in return, rewarded by the interesting drugstore bottles we found along the way.

Some of the discoveries in the mud had interesting bits of history embossed on them. For instance, one drugstore bottle had the name of a pharmacy in the former town of Albina, Oregon, now absorbed by Portland. We could also see the changes in the accepted abbreviation of Oregon: Ogn, Or, then Ore. In style, the Blake prescription, with flattened edges and unrecessed panels, seems to have been most popular during the late 1880s. On the other hand, a majority of our prescription bottles of the 1890s are of the oval styles.

An interesting contender of the late 1880s and 1890s was a subquadrate bottle. A cross section of the cylinder of such a bottle is like a piece of pie with the pointed half already eaten. These bottles were designed to be packed together in round shipping containers like barrels.

As the 20th century arrived, chain drugstores gained in popularity, and few of them continued to use embossed bottles. The Owl Drug Company, which began in 1892, was an exception. Its bottles, even with changes of ownership, continued to have the familiar owl emblem until 1933.

With the advent of the large drug company, the trend toward standardization, and new requirements, other prescription ware became common. In the early part of this century, the graduated prescription bottles (which have been available for decades) became prevalent. Most of these have what is known as a graduated double scale; one side shows oz., the other cc. Cork closures continued to dominate the scene until the late 1920s, although hand-blown, ground-top, screw-top closures were in use for some pill bottles by 1890.

Some of our earliest medicine bottles were plain and either smooth or 12-faceted, like these. Both were blown in hinged-bottom, two-piece molds. Pontilling indicates their ages at around 1850.

One interesting type of drugstore bottle was designed so it could be nested in barrels for shipping. These were used by Woodard Clarke, Druggists in Portland, Oregon, from 1881 to 1915, and by Blackman & Good, who were in business in Portland only from 1892 to 1894. Patent date on the base is May 15, '88.

This large medicinal bottle is embossed, "Jas. R. Nichols, Chemists, Boston." The Bostonian Society records show the company to have been in business from 1858 to the early 1870s. It was discovered in the Willamette near Oregon City.

Plain ball-neck panel prescription bottles like the one on the right were common in the medicine chests of the 1890s (authentic label added). They were replaced early this century with double graduated prescription ware (left) showing both oz. and cc.

118

These prescription-ware bottles are of the Blake style, popular in the late 1880s. Woodard Clarke & Co. bottle has an embossed metal seal on the cork. Note the OGN abbreviation for Oregon. (*Western & Eastern Treasures* Magazine photo)

Oval prescription bottles were also popular in the 1880s, becoming even more so in the 1890s. Albina merged with Portland in 1881, about the time Dr. Fisher opened his pharmacy. T. Shotbolt was a well-known early druggist in Victoria.

Right: Dark-amber bandage jars date from a time early in this century when gauze moistened with carbolic acid was in common use. The larger jar bears the initials of Bauer & Black. Minim measure is in the foreground.

Left: Among the chain drugstores, only Owl is known for its embossed bottles. These examples are circa 1910.

Right: A delight in cobalt blue glass, this Bromo Soda bottle was dug out of the mud complete with its matching glass dose measure.

The larger dispensing bottles are seldom found under water. Those were generally kept in the store or sick bay, and refilled when emptied. Such large bottles in my collection have come from trading, not diving. However, the medicinal and drugstore bottles that I have found have added interest, sometimes bits of history.

From the Cabins and Crews' Quarters

Life aboard ship went on as it did elsewhere. The ladies in the passenger cabins continued to use their perfumes and cosmetics; the men to douse their faces with aftershave, and even to partake of a little snuff. Shoes were shined and teeth were brushed. Ingredients for these activities became used up, and over the side the bottles went.

Perfume, polish, and milk-glass lotion bottles wind up in our diving bags occasionally. However, what seems most fascinating of these finds are the two extremes, the long-necked, slender Florida Water bottles that once held a sort of men's aftershave, and the short, squatty, often crude snuff containers. When we were diving at Yaquina City, a tiny, skinny bottle came to light from the mud, one that showed heavy embossing even through the marine growth. "Florida Water," the embossing read, "Murray & Lanman Druggists, New York." I immediately thought it some sort of patent medicine, perhaps using the fabled fountain of youth that was supposed to lie hidden in an unknown part of Florida. I was surprised to learn it was an aftershave lotion, liberally endowed with alcohol. Its diminutive size suggests it may have been a sample bottle. We have since found a number of graceful Florida Water bottles, but none so small as the one from Yaquina City.

One would not expect snuff bottles to be rare around the waterways, but we have found few. Perhaps the sailors were discouraged from using it, or was it too much the trademark of lumberjack and farmer? My collection includes only a couple of glass snuff jars, though I have found a couple more pottery containers in British Columbia that I have been told were snuff jars.

It would appear that while the ladies in the cabins were busily using their face creams, and tossing the milk-glass jars out the porthole, the pursers must have been busy making their entries, and the officers industriously writing the log, for ink bottles of all sizes are relatively common under water. Perhaps the most frequently found of this group are the little cone or bell jars that were used for ink and mucilage. They look something like the more popular, and older, umbrella ink bottle.

The waterways hold a number of the flat, square style of ink bottles that would seem more stable in a tossing vessel, and which have grooves around the upper edges to hold pens from rolling. These little boxy jars are in bottle-glass green, suggesting they are older than the often-clear cone and bell inks.

Master inks are also to be found, both in colored glass and in pottery. Pottery has appeared to be the preferred material for the ships that came into Port Townsend, Washington, for clay has predominated in the master inks from that location. It should be noted, however, that clay was frequently used for individual inks as well.

Although one of a kind, one of my most delightful acquisitions in the line of office relics is a little spirit lamp. So called because of the use of alcohol spirits, modern versions of these tiny items are still in use in some doctors' offices. The one that I discovered, still complete with its burner, wick, and ground-glass snuffer, had obviously been used at a desk. Spattered over its shoulders are drops of various colors of sealing wax. I wonder if some purser used this to seal his letters, or if some captain received his sealed orders from the owner of the ship, and my tiny lamp.

Glass for Marine and Industrial Use

We were in the dark, muddy waters of the Willamette River below Portland, following the beams of our diving flashlights, when we came upon some massive bits of bottle-collecting material. These were obviously, even half-buried in the silt, the size of object one places in a corner for a terrarium instead of on a shelf with the rest of the bottle collection.

Snuff containers typically stand no higher than 4 inches, have no significant necks, and are topped with simple, rolled lips. The pottery jar from Quadra Island, British Columbia, seems to fit this description, though the black glass example on the right has the more common boxy shape. It has a refired (heat polished) pontil mark.

Shown above are three cabin-type bottles recovered from under water. In the center is a Vanstan's Statena bottle, which held a kind of glue. Flanking it are two polish bottles, one embossed, "Whittemore, Boston, U.S.A.," and the other plain.

By the 1890s, milk-glass or opal glass made by the pressed-glass method rather than blowing—and with nickel-plated brass or aluminum screw caps—had become popular. Similar styles were continued into the present time, so identification of the old examples is difficult. An 1890s catalog lists these (left to right) as tall ointment, fancy cold cream, fluted ointment, and screw-cap urn styles.

Our waterways hold many ink containers. The master ink (left) was encountered in Tillamook Bay, Oregon; the little cylinder, embossed "Underwood's Inks," was recovered from Quathiaski Cove, British Columbia. The pair of square bottles, embossed "L.H. Thomas Co., Chicago" on their bases, were found at Portland, Oregon, and Gowland Harbor, British Columbia.

In old glassware catalogs these are called (left to right): cone ink, bell mucilage, and umbrella ink. The cone ink bears "Carter's" on its base; the bell mucilage is marked, "Sanfords."

Pottery was often used for ink containers in the 19th century. The individual inkwell is unmarked, but the master ink jar in the center bears the names of P & J Arnold (ink merchants) and J. Bourne & Son, who operated Denby Pottery in the 1850s. The smaller master ink on the right, stamped "Carter's Inks," is later and has a pouring spout added in the lip.

Florida Water was seemingly synonymous with men's toiletries in the 19th century. Embossed Florida Water bottles could be purchased from glassware catalogs and filled locally. Contents would thus vary. A few, like the sample bottle found at the former seaport of Yaquina City, had the name of the drugstore included in the embossing.

The little spirit lamp from Portland, Oregon, has drops of sealing wax clinging to its shoulder. Apparently it sat on a desk and was used to seal letters. On the right is a desk inkwell found at Port Townsend, Washington.

This forerunner of our glass gallon jug had a puffy neck to support a cork closure. Note the deep, wide groove for the metal band, which once was the attachment for a wire-bale-and-wooden handle. Such handles permitted the use of the whole hand in carrying. Date of manufacture is circa 1910.

Some of the more colorful pottery items the author has found in the Willamette River near Portland have been the antique toothpaste containers. Rarely were lid and jar encountered together under water, for the lids merely slipped on instead of being secured by threads like nearly all modern containers. Lids and jars at left and center seem to match. The center example is turned to show underglaze printing on the base. To the right is the author's favorite, a lid with lettering and design in hues of olive and gold, but, alas—without the jar.

The larger of these chemical jars was probably made in the 1880s. In this case the "whittle mark" pattern was probably caused by a cold mold rather than the chisel marks of a wooden mold. From faint embossing on the base of the medium-sized (quart) bottle can be discerned "Platt's Chlorides Disinfectant." It, and the dark-amber Mallingkrodt bottle, are also likely from the 1880s, though later in that decade.

The larger of these chemical jars contains an unknown green oily liquid and is embossed "B. K. H. Company, Germany." It appears to have been blown in a dip mold and hand worked at the neck and shoulder, a definite possibility since the embossing is on the base. Center bottle, made by T.C. Wheaton Glass Co., contains medical alcohol. The label on the Whitall Tatum manufactured bottle on the right indicates concentrated sulphuric acid. Center and right-hand examples were blown in three-piece molds.

Early electrical reservoirs were wet cells contained in ceramic crocks or glass jars. Such units saw marine, industrial, and occasional household use.

The oldest Edison Special Battery Oil bottles were green and shaped like the example on the left. It was found at Blind Channel, British Columbia. Center bottle, looking like oval prescription ware, came from Nehalem Bay. On the right is a later example, designed for a metal crown cap; this was a gift from Pete Craddock. All three bottles bear the embossed facsimile of Thomas A. Edison's signature.

Since pioneer railroad and telegraph lines followed the waterways, the diver-collector's bag of glass and ceramic objects is apt to include some communications items that are not nautical. The ridged cylindrical insulators in the foreground are typical of early ship use.

This telephone, along with its separate magneto and bells, was found in the Willamette River. It is interesting to consider the pressures in an office even when this type of phone was in use. Just picture the former owner saying, "If that phone rings one more time. . . ."—and there that phone was, out in the channel.

We had encountered a group of containers once used for chemicals, lubricants, and other liquids that had made the wheels of industry turn, or the ship's machinery to function smoothly. At this location there were so many gallon and half-gallon containers in clear and amber glass that we quit picking them up. A few earlier jugs, about one of each kind apiece, was about all we wanted. After all, being nearly filled with mud, they were pretty heavy.

Looking them over later, we did find them interesting. The gallons with handles were of an early machine-made type, which were of a straight but slightly swollen neck style intended only for cork closure. Strangely, even those with handles cast in the glass still had the heavy indentation around the base of the neck—a groove shown in 1890s glassware catalogs as being for metal bands to support carrying handles. Apparently the wire-and-wooden handle was used for easier carrying (it accommodated the whole hand) while the glass-ring handle was only for pouring. Smaller jugs, in quart and two-quart size, had only the groove for the band to attach a wire-and-wooden handle.

We have found earlier chemical jugs, hand blown and finished, a few with interesting "whittle-mark" patterns which some collectors feel are imparted by hand-carved molds. When an embossed one was found, at Port Townsend, Washington, we hoped finally to be able to pinpoint the use of one such jug. It was marked, *Mallingkrodt Chemical Works, St. Louis*. The Mallingkrodt Company is still in business, so we wrote to them about the embossed amber bottle we found. When the reply came, however, regret was expressed that they could not be specific. Chemical bottles are used for a wide variety of products, and our unusual embossed bottle could have contained any one of the list of their products they provided for us. Their principal products, though, seemed to be cleaning and disinfecting chemicals.

A diver occasionally finds a smaller chemical bottle, likely a pint or smaller, with a narrow neck and glass stopper ground to fit. Many of these were made by the Wheaton Glass Company, and earlier ones show the markings of a three-piece mold. If the contents are inside, the diver should exercise extreme care—often these were used for concentrated acids. A dangerous chemical could have been disposed of by throwing it over the side.

From time to time we have come upon oil bottles under water. Yes, oil once came in glass; cans were not economical until modern crimping was developed around 1920. The oldest identifiable as oil bottles were found in Puget Sound, and are embossed "Sperm Sewing Machine Oil." They are panel prescription style, and the finish suggests early 1890s. We wondered why so many sewing-machine oil bottles would be in the water, until we learned that sperm oil was also used to lubricate the pumps for early hard-hat divers.

It was below the bluff in Quathiaski Cove, British Columbia, where the refuse of an old homestead had been dumped, that we encountered the largest number of oil bottles. Not only did we find several "3-in-1" bottles, but I found the only "Winches-chester" gun-oil bottle I have ever seen. R. I. Frost, Curator of the Buffalo Bill Museum, which includes the Winchester Gun Museum, confirmed that the Winchester Company did, indeed, market its gun oil in glass jars from 1909 until 1925. Mine is likely one of the early ones, since it is hand finished. (I have since added a touch of desert amethyst color to it by leaving it in the sun on the patio roof this past summer.)

In Nehalem Bay another interesting kind of oil bottle first came to our attention. This was the "Special Battery Oil" bottle with the signature of Thomas A. Edison embossed on one side. Such glassware contained oil that was poured over the electrolyte of the Edison-Lelande cells to prevent evaporation. Shortly afterward, pottery battery jars were discovered, one of them in green glass with a ground lip. We felt these were artifacts of the wireless sets that guided tugs and lumber schooners into the ports of Wheeler and Nehalem, fired the early combustion engines, and lighted primitive electric lamps.

Nehalem is the only place where we have been fortunate enough to find complete wet cells, but remains litter the ports throughout the Northwest. Most were in white crocks of about half-gallon capacity, which were seemingly easily damaged. Broken ones have been noted in Nehalem, Alsea, and various other bays. A few were apparently used or re-used as dry cells, although the only one I have seen complete with contents, tar covering, and posts from the electrodes was picked up by a diving companion in Port Townsend, Washington.

Many other industrial and marine items are there to find, objects like glass and ceramic insulators, fire extinguishers, and even an occasional telephone. It's a grab bag; the diver never knows what to expect.

PART III.
POTTERY AND PORCELAIN FROM THE SEA

CHAPTER 7.

GALLEY WARE AND RELATED OBJECTS

Ships also, of course, carried dishes and other pottery items, many of which bear a distinctive mark of the sea. Chandlers stocked dishes, cups, mugs, bowls and such ware that were best suited to the characteristics of the galley and the ship's mess. Consequently, our waterways contain pottery or chinaware specific to the waters, but much more that shared use on land and sea.

Steamer Ware

Early in what became annual diving holidays in British Columbia, we became intrigued by objects carrying the green emblem and white anchor of the old Union Steamship Company. I was in Heriot Bay, which had been one of the ports of call of the steamers, when I found my first Union relic. It was a simple white cup with two green stripes around the bowl and a green scroll containing the initials, "U. S. S. C⁰ of B. C. Ltd." A short time later I came upon part of a dinner plate with an oval belt-like garter design encircling the letters "U S S C." I was hooked.

The following summer, I met Peter Craddock, who lives near Heriot Bay and shares my enthusiasm for Union Steamship relics. Together, we tried diving other former steamer ports, Pete guiding and tending the boat while my diving companions and I searched the sea floor below.

Granite Bay revealed nothing, but at Whaletown we discovered two Union Steamship-Estates mugs, some cups, and two creamers. These were of a different pattern, an apparently more common one with a white anchor in the center.

During two more years we made special trips back to British Columbia for expeditions up the inside passage to other prior ports, places now abandoned or nearly so, where the gold mines are closed and fallen in, or where the loggers have moved on. The diving has resulted in nice collections of steamer dishes, platters, cups, saucers, and other mementos. Despite a plague of engine troubles, these have been some of the most memorable diving trips I have ever taken.

In this case, the steamship markings made the finds special. However, a knowledge of pottery itself and the markings used by the craftsmen who created it provides added pleasure in the discoveries. For instance, my oldest piece of Union china is a platter made by John Maddock & Sons, England. The company that made it has an interesting history, beginning in 1839 as Maddock & Seddon, Burslem, Staffordshire, England. The name became John Maddock & Sons in 1855, but the specific emblem marking my platter was used in 1896.

The base of the object was imprinted before firing with a "9" to show which worker shaped it, and a still-unexplained "Tax" with an impression that could be a crown. Maddock's lion-and-scroll emblem is just above the work "Vitrified," which means the dish had been fired to the intensity that would make the clay fused and hardened "like glass." It also carries an implication of clearness, and some such wares are translucent to a degree.

A significance of Maddock's 1896 emblem is that it dates the platter to a time just seven years after the formation of the Union Steamship Company. Since the steamship emblem is USSC (omitting the "Ltd."), an early mark of the Union company, we have verification of the approximate age of the item. To us, this ties in nicely with the discovery of the chinaware in Rock Bay, one of the early ports of call of the line.

Early Ships' Ware

In this case, it was the historical connection with the Union
line, not the age of the chinaware, that fascinated us. Actually,
in terms of history of pottery, the platter is made by modern
methods. We have found much older chinaware in the former
sailing ports like Port Ludlow, Washington. There we encountered heavy bowls and dishes that are of earlier methods of
manufacture, though most are unmarked. These relics of sail,
besides their pottery composition, have some interesting differences. Deep and heavy, they would slip around less as the vessel
rolled or heeled over onto the larboard tack. The dinner plates
were also heavy, and deep as well, somewhat like a wide soup
bowl. Boiled potatoes and peas should have been less apt to roll
out of them in a pitching ship.

Another reason for the heaviness of older ships' chinaware is
that it was softer. Methods of firing to a greater hardness were
not yet discovered. Such dishes were porous where not protected
by glaze, and were easily chipped and cracked. A good example
of the type of composition—one that most people are familiar
with because of renewed popularity—is Delftware (written delft
if produced in England instead of Holland). It is recognized by
its blue free-flowing designs painted into the hot tin glaze.
Delft, along with clay-colored stoneware and unglazed red ware
(often in imitation of Chinese or Japanese motifs), were
common through the 18th century.

The use of salt glaze, which people in the United States asso-
ciate with whiskey jugs, began its popularity around 1730. It is
recognizable by the pitted surface of the glaze, at times so extreme it became known as "orange peel" texture. Salt glaze was
easy for the small potter to use, for it simply consisted of throwing some salt into the kiln as it reached firing temperature. The
salt broke down chemically in the intense heat and settled over
the contents of the kiln, covering the ware with a hard glaze. In
England, salt-glazed ware was replaced by the smoother cream-
colored earthenware called "Queensware" by around 1770. We

This Myott Son & Co. English dish had just been picked up at Nehalem, Oregon. Markings suggest it was made around 1907. (Paul Cooper photo, reprinted courtesy of *Diver* Magazine)

Union Steamship relics like these lured us back to British Columbia and the coves that served as ports along the gold-rush route. The circa 1896 platter is in the background. The mug and creamer were made by Grindley Hotel Ware around 1908. Grindley later became part of Globe Pottery, England.

Grindley pottery of England supplied many of the cups and dishes that were found in the waterways of British Columbia. Some of our Union Steamship relics are marked "Grindley Hotel Ware" and the name of the supplier, "Cassidy's Ltd., Montreal, Vancouver, Toronto, & Winnepeg." It is appropriate that this mug, recovered at Shoal Bay, be marked with a Grindley emblem linking that company with the sea.

Dishes from the days of sail, these appear to be among the oldest chinaware we have recovered from former sailing ports we have visited. Plain and heavy stoneware, both the bowl and the dish are quite thick, the dish deeper by far than customary dinner plates. They have no maker's markings or indication of country of origin impressed or imprinted on their bases. Items like these were often supplied to ships during the early part of the 19th century, before the harder ironstone was developed.

would, therefore, not expect many salt-glazed objects to be found among ships' dishes in the Pacific Northwest.

Queensware was continued for many decades, and Wedgewood was heavily involved in its production. It is logical to assume that examples found their way to this area in ships' galleys, and some may have been made here for local chandlers. One of our sailing-ship bowls appears to be made of this cream-colored ware, though there are no markings that would help verify this.

Low-fired Stoneware (not to be confused with "Ironstone") of a refined type was used well into the 19th century. Some low-fired pottery apparently continued to be made even into the late 19th century, at least in North America, for some of the dishes we found in Rock Bay—and which appeared to be late 19th century—were porous beneath the glaze. As they sat on the shelf back home in my basement, sea water continued for several months to seep out through the cracks and evaporate, until little delicate walls of salt crystals stood above the cracks.

Ironstone

One spring we slipped into the water at Port Gamble, Washington, to see what we might find. It had been a lumber port since 1853, and we felt it could be well stocked with bottles and other relics. What we discovered was a good supply from ships' galleys. Many bottles were found, but so were quite a few "Ironstone" objects. Plates, saucers, and cups were recovered, along with some nice glass relics like a master salt dish and a plain but pontil-marked cruet.

The oldest dish obtained at Port Gamble, as far as we could tell from markings, was a plain saucer (no pattern) with the base imprinted "Iron Stone, DAVENPORT." The Davenport company existed from 1793 to 1881, Davenport Limited from 1881 to 1887. What narrowed the dating on the saucer was the pre-Victorian royal coat of arms above the name. This was used on Iron Stone objects from about 1815 to 1837. The saucer was probably old when it was lost overboard.

Other dishes were marked "Ironstone" and "Royal Ironstone," and were more typical of the early days of the port. Most dishes and related objects carried on ships after 1850 could be classed as "Ironstone." This is a much harder, nonporous pottery made vitreous by firing to around 1300°C. It is still being made and used, though the "Ironstone" labeling was seemingly dropped after a few decades in favor of "Vitreous."

Other markings that denote ironstone-type pottery are "Stone China" and "Semi Porcelain." These were less frequently used, and the only time I have seen "Semi Porcelain" on a piece was when I picked up a Wood & Sons vase in Gowland Harbor, B.C.

One might wonder what a vase was doing in the sea (I certainly have), but I have encountered a number of them. While diving in the Siletz River of the Oregon coast, I found a carnival-glass vase; and at Yaquina City, Oregon, a prized art-glass vase was uncovered. There have been a few others, though not as old as the circa-1840 Wood & Sons vase, nor as valuable as the art glass. One other that is worthy of mention is a circa-1860 bisque (unglazed pottery) vase with hand-sculptured roses that was discovered in the Willamette River at Sauvie Island.

My only theory about the vases lies with the wives of sea captains. Some masters of vessels took their wives along, and I am sure the ladies were inclined to brighten the cabin with flowers at every opportunity. My theory doesn't explain how they came to be over the side, however.

Pottery Designs

There have been a number of times and places where it was the chinaware that provided the thrills of discovery. Several years ago we were diving in Oregon's Siletz River, drifting along with the outgoing tide, and struggling to keep out of the entangling limbs of waterlogged trees that lined the channel. We started diving the area in search of the commercial fishing boat that had sunk at its moorings and been swept down the river. At one point we found the compass, at another the brass bow light and a few insignifcant items. This was the second day of working our way down the river.

Suddenly, scattered about the bottom, we came upon various kinds of dishes. All of the items were flat, however: dinner plates, lids of bowls, saucers, things that would cling to the smooth river floor. The first object to be picked up was a salad plate with a floral-design transfer printed over the glaze. Then, I turned over a dinner plate and discovered it was blue Willow Ware. Several more plates were among the things lying in the mud. Our theory is that a cabin had been swept away by some nearly forgotten flood and had broken up at this spot, strewing the housewares along the floor of the Siletz. The current had carried along the bulkier objects, but left the dishes.

Our Willow Ware carries the mark of "Royal China." This was the pottery mark of E. Hughes & Co. of Fenton, Staffordshire, England. Hughes began his pottery production in 1889, and since our examples do not carry the 1891 Tariff Act requiring markings of country of origin, we can assume these are early samples of Hughes' ware. Perhaps it is also significant that M. Seller of Portland was advertising "Willow Ware" at about that same time.

Another significance of this ware is the blue-and-white pattern in imitation of oriental designs. The earliest coloring discovered which could withstand the heat of vitreous firing and could thus be placed under the glaze was a blue derived from cobalt. Early durable under-glaze patterns were blue. A saucer that was found with the blue Willow Ware had transfer-printed decorations which had been refired at a lower temperature—and were wearing off. In contrast, the Willow Ware showed no signs of wear or fading.

The use of cobalt-blue under-glaze patterns enjoyed long popularity. An example picked up at the same location in British Columbia as the ship's compass dates from around 1910.

From these experiences, and a little study, we have come to pay attention to the pottery as well as brass relics and bottles we encounter in our diving. Observation has shown some patterns of interest. Coffee cups and mugs are the most commonly found pottery ware. They were doubtless placed on the gunwale and became the casualty of a careless move or unexpected roll of the ship.

In the waterways we also find many bowls that resemble mugs without handles. We encountered them at Port Ludlow and Port Gamble, Washington, and Newport, Oregon, to name a few places. Ask an old sailor what they were for, and you get the same answer, "soup." Perhaps the makers were influenced by the oriental trade, for the items are somewhat like enlarged Chinese soup bowls, but I am sure they were also desirable as hand warmers on cold nights. I can almost visualize a seaman standing watch, warming his hands with a soup bowl perched on the gunwale.

One of the first things we do when we find a pottery item is to turn it over, scratch away the encrustations or mud, and look at the label. We have been interested in the maker, and also the chandler or supplier. Often the cup or dish was made for a particular supply house and the markings include the name of the chandler.

One label brought about an amusing incident. Among the various relics of the deep from Nehalem, Oregon, was a fairly deep-cupped dinner plate marked with a large lion-and-unicorn-surrounded shield emblem and "Charles Meakin, Hanley, England." This printed mark was used in Eastwood Pottery, Hanley, Staffordshire, only from 1883 to 1889. It was so impressive that when we set up a display in the window of the Nehalem Bay Trading Company we placed the dish with the emblem up.

On one afternoon, as I stood visiting with Roy Harwood—one of the owners—a matronly woman stopped abruptly, and then without a word, solemnly stomped in through the front door, stretched over the rest of the display, grabbed the dish and turned it over. Almost groaning, she returned it and, still without a word, stomped back out of the store. Sorry, lady, ships' dishes were normally plain.

This blue-pattern Wedgwood & Co. "Countryside" dish was found at the site of the capsizing that gave up the ship's compass. It bears some barnacle remains, plus some chips that may have come from its tumble to the sea floor. Its maker, Wedgwood & Co. (Ltd. added in 1900), was founded in 1835 by Enoch Wedgwood, and should not be confused with the better-known Josiah Wedgwood, whose successors still use the mark, "Wedgwood."

Port Gamble, Washington, which has operated continuously as a lumber port since 1853, has yielded a substantial amount of ironstone china. Both the dish and saucer are plain like most galley ware. The saucer, turned to show the "Iron Stone, Davenport" and pre-Victorian Royal Arms, is the oldest piece found by us in the bay. It was old before it was lost overboard, dating from before 1837.

This circa 1889 Willow Ware dish, recovered from the Siletz River, is a good example of blue under-glaze decoration. The pattern imitates an original motif, but the dish was made in England by E. Hughes & Co. The Hughes mark of "Royal China" is shown in the inset. It, too, is blue under the glaze.

This dish from Gowland Harbor, British Columbia, is one of the few we have found in the shipping lanes that have appreciable decoration. The dish dates from the 1920s, but the pattern is widely copied in hotel and restaurant ware today. Emblem of the Newport Pottery Co., its maker, is shown.

In size and shape, these items look like handleless mugs, but were used for soup from the galley.

Cups and mugs are the most abundant forms of chinaware encountered under water. Illustrated above are examples from various port areas. Most marked items show pottery companies in England.

Dishes, cups, saucers, and creamers decorated with blue-and-white checkered flags and bands turned up at Willamette River steamer ports. These examples were collected at Canemah. Creamer on the right is turned to show Wood & Sons marking and "Oregon."

This oblong bowl from Quathiaski Cove, British Columbia, is misleading in appearance. It is decorated in under-glaze blue that appears 19th century, as does the style of the dish. However, the company that produced it was in business from 1890 to 1931. This item is circa 1910.

147

These decorated items were recovered from Quathiaski Cove. The design is underglaze green transfer-printed. Markings indicate they were made by Grimwade's (Ltd.) around 1906. The UHP stands for Upper Hanley Pottery, which is written out in some of the markings after 1906.

The serving platters and bowls used in the late 19th century were also plain. But, as we entered the 20th century, ships' ware took on a new perspective. It was decorated, but conservatively. Cups, mugs, dishes, and serving bowls were often encircled with a few stripes. These could be of more than one width, either a broad plus a narrow stripe, or a broad stripe surrounded by narrow ones. The USSC favored two narrow stripes, always in green. In fact, green was the predominant color—appropriate for the sea.

Perhaps it was the freshwater influence that brought out the use of blue instead of green trim, for, as we dived the early steamer ports of the Willamette River we encountered the unique "Oregon" patterned chinaware. Like the steamship ware of British Columbia, it was decorated with two narrow bands around the edges. However, the bands were blue-and-white checkered and interrupted at opposite sides with checkered flags.

There were several companies that operated steamers on the Willamette and incorporated "Oregon" into their name: the Oregon Steam Navigation Company, the Oregon Railway & Navigation Company, and the Oregon Steamship Company. We tend to attribute this chinaware, though, to the latter company.

The Oregon Steamship Company came into existence in 1870 when Ben Holladay bought out the People's Transporation Company. He had been the promoter of the Oregon & California Railroad which had just initiated its runs through Oregon City. Ben did things with a flourish, and would have ordered distinctive chinaware on which to serve his steamboat passengers.

Further evidence suggesting this origin is to be found in the fact that the greatest abundance of "Oregon" chinaware was discovered at Canemah, where the *Albany, Shoo Fly,* and *McMinnville* were built and which they claimed as home port. At the time of discovery, the dishes were scattered amid relics of the O & C Railroad, Ben's other venture. A final point is that one of the Oregon Steamship Company's vessels, though not on the Willamette run, was named *Oregon*.

Other dishes found in the Willamette ports were undecorated, utilitarian items. Only where the port areas overlapped into locations where householders dumped the garbage down the bank did we find attractively decorated dishes. These were usually broken.

Chinaware was virtually absent from the log-rafting areas of the river. Instead, we found numerous enamelware items. Most common were the coffee pots of gray enamel swirled with streaks of black. A few still had lids, though the hinges had rusted from most. Cups of gray, white, or blue were frequently encountered, dishes and kettles at other times. It would seem that enamelware replaced pottery on the tugs that replaced the steamers on the river. Competition from the railroad had eliminated the steamer routes by the 1880s, a time when enamelware was also becoming popular.

In Quathiaski Cove, British Columbia, a number of nicely patterned English china dishes were discovered. However, we had been told that things from the homestead above the bluff had been thrown there. What we picked up on this occasion were the last remaining pieces of sets, items that no longer fitted in with the family pattern. Regardless, we enjoyed finding the discards of years ago, even though their decoration made them stand out from the typical ships' chinaware we had previously acquired.

There have been other items from the deep that seem out of character. These are the porcelain objects from the salons of passing ships. Porcelain is another high-temperature-fired chinaware, with the distinguishing characteristic of being translucent. It is vitreous in the true meaning. Though made of clay and petuntse (a Chinese feldspathic mineral) it resembles milk glass. I think of it mostly as being in the cabinets of fancy homes, but we found several delicate porcelain teacups in the ports once visited by steamers. They must have been used to serve tea to the lady passengers.

These objects were made in Japan and found in British Columbia. The dish is fairly soft, of low-fired material that has chipped. However, the cup is one of several made of durable, translucent porcelain. It is patterned inside as well as outside with an intricate blue pattern.

The floors of the old steamer ports of British Columbia are littered with teapots. Accompanying them are a scattering of bone china cups, probably once used in the steamer salons. Most are plain, pastel-colored, and unmarked. However, the elaborate blue-and-white example is marked "Copeland, Spode's Tower."

This cream pitcher, recovered from the Willamette River, appeared on the tables of the once-fashionable Portland Hotel (torn down a few decades ago).

Base of the pitcher shows that the Portland Hotel, a show-place at the time, had imported its chinaware from Limoges, France.

The channel at Nehalem Bay yielded this plain pitcher. Its base was faintly marked with a bell topped by what appeared to be an eagle head. Lettering on the bell emblem is "The Colonial."

Among our favorite vases of the waterways are this dark-red-and-black art glass example from Yaquina City, and a barnacled carnival-glass vase from Siletz Bay.

This little milk-glass pitcher was originally plucked from the Willamette River mud above Oregon City as a plaything for the author's young daughter. Then we spotted a patent date of Nov. 3, 1870, and it was a plaything no longer.

We were primarily looking for b when we came upon this cruet master salt dish in Gamble Bay, W ington. The cruet has a pontil where it was held to fashion the ho the master salt dish shows its age i innumerable little chips from s that dipped into its contents.

Much silverware has been recovered from beneath the waters, but the only well-preserved pieces in author's collection are those at the lower part of the photo—and they were gifts.

It would be interesting to know the story behind this demitasse cup and spoon discovered at Port Townsend, Washington.

That isn't a bad assumption. In the same ports we came upon many teapots and several other teacups made of porcelain-like material, bone china. Like our porcelain trophies, they are small, delicate, and sometimes brightly colored or ornately decorated. Bone china is not translucent, however. It is formed of an opaque clay body, one of the ingredients of which is bone ash.

There always seems to be a miscellany of galley items around old port areas. In addition to the usual dishes, Nehalem Bay yielded an ironstone-type pitcher. The Willamette River held a little cream pitcher from the tables of the now-torn-down Portland Hotel. The same location contained a pottery spitoon with lion's head decorations and inevitable tobacco stains. From Brinnon, Washington, came a dish whose checked surface had shed its maker's mark but not the "18 K Gold" bands.

Not all the galley ware has been of pottery or porcelain. Mixed among the cups, dishes, and such have been pitchers and other items of pressed glass. Such things have not been as common, but they, too, have added interest to our diving.

The galley ware that suffers most from the sea, and even from immersion in fresh water, is the silverware. Our metal detectors have located an assortment of knives, forks, and spoons, but most have lost too much of their silver plating to be restorable. At this time, the only really nice silverware objects in my collection are two spoons some traveler carried away from ocean liners, and which came to me as gifts from a friend, Don Bergseng.

Perhaps it is partly because I have always eaten well while at sea, but I have come to appreciate the galley relics I have acquired.

CHAPTER 8.

RELICS FROM CHINA

The sea and the Orient combine to provide many pleasures of beachcombing to the west coast of North America. Not only do we still experience the annual rush for storm-driven glass floats, but history records the occasional arrival of derelict oriental ships upon our coast. The existence of Chinese pottery shards among Indian artifacts, and an ancient Oriental-appearing stone bridge, add to our mysteries from the Orient.

More identifiable than the shards, and more varied than the glass floats, are the relics left along our waterways by Chinese laborers who came to this country for jobs, and hopefully a better life. Chinese workers not only built the railroads during the transcontinental race in the early 1880s, and worked the gold mines, they also served upon the waterways and labored at the edge of the sea. Chinese are known to have been employed as cooks and mess attendants in ships along the Inside Passage through British Columbia and Alaskan waters. Many more worked in fish canneries at the docks. It is logical, then, that they would add discarded bits of the Orient to the floor of many a harbor.

British Columbia Discoveries

We were particularly hopeful of finding Chinese relics in British Columbia. Pete Craddock had dug a number of nice, brown pottery items, and showed us where the Chinese once lived at the Lucky Jim gold mine. There wasn't much left at the mine but walls of log buildings and parts of the pole frames where Chinese miners lived in their tents. We hoped the cove at nearby Granite Bay would yield some artifacts, but when we dived it, all we found was soft mud.

At nearby Heriot Bay, we found a couple of Chinese bottles, tinted a jade green and looking like roughly made pop bottles. Their bases contained the only embossing—not much for display. These had probably been discards from Chinese cooks, as the bay had once been a steamer port.

We searched the floor of the harbor at Whaletown, a former steamer port on Cortes Island, and discovered, among the clutter of bottles and dishes, one pottery ginger jar. The discoveries had still been single items, and our interest wasn't satisfied with that. One more possibility remained before the end of our vacation in British Columbia, and that was the old cannery site in Quathiaski Cove. The cannery and dock had burned, but the relics under water should have been intact. Perhaps they were, but they were totally buried by layers of circa-1920 beer bottles. The cannery workers may have been of Chinese heritage, but their beverage preference was obviously Canadian beer.

Oregon Discoveries

It was back home in Portland where we finally located the "right spot." An unusual winter drought gave us unheard-of visibility in the Willamette—and a tip about a location where Portland's garbage was once incinerated along the river-bank placed us there. At first we encountered American glass and broken bits of Chinese dishes and pottery. Then, as the water became colder it cleared, and we reached the 30-foot depth at the floor of the river. One small area, not over 75 feet in diameter and starting 50 feet out from the edge of the sloping bank, contained a veritable bonanza of Oriental pottery. The first sight of the bottom, made following a flashlight beam down an old piling, revealed three objects: a tiger whiskey, a soy sauce jug, and an wide-mouth pot.

One of the last items to be retrieved from the relic hole in the Willamette was this holder for stick incense. The upper half is hollow to act as a holder; two discs were intended to catch the ashes.

In Heriot Bay, British Columbia, Chinese liquor bottles were found, made of glass with a jade-green tint and crudely resembling a pop bottle. However, these examples have bubbles in the glass and misshapen necks. Smaller bottle on the right is a Chinese medicine bottle, often erroneously called an opium bottle.

Once the place was detected, pottery continued to come to the surface until the supply was seemingly exhausted. Almost from this single location we arrived at a Chinese relic collection. The most thrilling items were two huge (five gallons and larger) rounded pottery containers, but there were enough tiger whiskey jugs, soy-sauce containers, wide-mouth jars, and other artifacts to get a pretty good idea of the Chinese discards to be found in Northwest waters. From these discoveries, and follow-up study, we were able to arrive at some conclusions.

Our huge clay jugs, we were told by people in the Chinese-American community, had been used as bulk shipping containers for liquids like soy sauce destined for stores. They have been more readily available in San Francisco, where some have been sold for the maufacture of very impressive lamps. Being handmade, they are variable in size.

The smaller soy-sauce containers, though still hand-formed, were more consistent. Our examples varied from 40 to 44 ounces in capacity, and were all of rounded shape. Pete Craddock had given me a square soy-sauce container he dug on Vancouver Island. It had two world globes stamped into a side, and some Chinese characters that translated roughly into, "World Wide Exporting Company." None of our soy-sauce containers had inscriptions.

The wide-mouth pots fell into two size categories. These were basically around 17-ounce and 40-ounce groupings. The use was something like our glass fruit jars in pint and quart sizes—for a wide variety of foodstuffs.

Tiger whiskeys, the research showed, were a little taller and more slender at the time ours were made (1880s and 1890s), and held a couple more ounces than later ones we studied. They were imported into this country again after Prohibition ended, but these are embossed "Federal Law Forbids Sale or Re-use of this Bottle," and are of the 4/5-quart size. The newer examples were also a rather uniform brown color, while older ones from the Willamette were finer glazed (glossier) in tones of brown, copper, and steel blue.

Bringing large pottery jugs up to the boat was a difficult task. The first to be discovered was turned over and filled with air to float it to the surface, but the second was full of hard-packed mud and had to be carried up a steep bank under water. Shown is the first one. (Don Bergseng photo)

This heavy iron pot was encountered among the Chinese pottery objects. When found, it contained a mass of bones from a large bird, perhaps a goose.

All the soy sauce jugs found in the Willamette dive were rounded like the example on the left. This one had been dropped, a hole broken in the base, and the contents apparently lost, for the lightly glazed, thin clay plug is still in the spout. Square soy-sauce container on the right was dug on Vancouver Island by Pete Craddock. (*Old Bottle* Magazine photo)

Several small containers were found among the Chinese relics in the Willamette. The little crock on the left is made of brown clay and glazed with runny dark-blue material. The white crock in the center is glazed only on the inside and has a tiny face on each handle knob. On the right is a very thin, rounded clay bowl with runny brown glaze.

Dishes found in the Willamette site included this crude clay Chinese dish on the left and several (all damaged) blue-glazed and decorated dishes as shown in the center and right. None had the country of origin stamped on their bases.

Ginger jars are distinctly rounded with a short lip (often unglazed). Most are attractively decorated, thus retained or sold, not discarded where they might be found by divers.
(G. Quackenbush photo)

The common Chinese wide-mouthe
pots, which somewhat resembled Bo
ton bean containers, could be divide
into two size groups. A variety of foo
stuffs came in them, similar to what
available in present pint and quart gla
jars. (*Old Bottle* Magazine photo)

Tiger whiskey jugs from the 1880s and 1890s are generally more slender and taller than later examples. The jug on the left, found in the Willamette River, has a copper-tone glossy glaze and holds a few more ounces than the post-Prohibition whiskey jug on the right. (*Old Bottle* Magazine photo)

The Willamette yielded smaller items as well: an opium pipe bowl, a little rounded brown-glazed container for paste foods (the top of which would have completed its ball appearance was not found), a 4-ounce blue-glazed crock, an 8-ounce white crock with tiny faces as handle knobs, and a 6-inch-high tiered holder for stick incense.

EPILOGUE

Where Next?

The water shimmers, quiet and placid in the summer sun. Green leaves of the tender plants that spring up and overgrow the beach reach to the water's edge at high tide. Annuals from the sandy soil and young shoots from nearby willows almost hide the bleached bones of a wooden hull cast upon the shore. Forgotten are the winter storms.

Yet, beneath the mirror-like surface were found the relics of disaster. It was here that a brass ship's compass, some dishes, cups, and other mementos of capsizing were gathered. Where else, beneath the now-quiet waters, lie the treasures left by maritime events?

If a lifetime were available for the sole purpose of diving and beachcombing, I could never reach all the fascinating places I have heard of, or places where charts and other information suggest a wealth of relics from the deep. Even close to home there are many unexplored locations.

A half-hour drive from my house is the Sauvie Island (Willamette River) location where we found the array of Chinese relics. The portion we searched thoroughly would be contained in a 75-by-75-foot square. Just beyond it is a place where a Hudson's Bay Company outpost is said to have existed. This may well be correct, for that company is known to have established the dairy industry on the island and traded with the Indians living there. We simply haven't had time to check it out.

In another direction, less than an hour from the house, is Butteville on the Willamette River. Another Hudson's Bay trading post stood there, and steamers continued to stop at the community long after the Bay had moved. We have been to Butteville, but became intrigued with the debris of the steamer explosion, so didn't fully explore the river alongside the old port.

Yes, a steamer exploded near Butteville, for the river bottom yielded burst tubing, pieces of boiler plate, broken firebricks, grating, the firebox door, and the stoker. Scattered about the river nearby were wagon parts, plowshares, hundreds of unused bricks, and fired clay pipe. From the markings on the pipe we know it was being shipped between 1898 and 1911, for that was when Western Clay Manufacturing Company, the company that made and marked it, was in business. From the glassware and pottery it would appear closer to 1898, but time hasn't been sufficient to complete the search or study records of damaged steamers. We have never been into the depths of the 45-foot-deep narrow canyon that comprises the channel at that point. Does it hide the hull of the steamer? We don't know, for we were without adequate lights when we were exploring the area, and could not see well in the gloom between the steep walls of the narrow channel.

On one dive, I hooked up an automobile sealed-beam headlight to the 12-volt system of our boat via a series of extension cords whose connections were sealed with wetsuit cement. It worked adequately until the air tank became empty and I tried to return to the surface. Then I discovered I had passed under a log or another unseen obstruction so the cord was looped stoutly around something on the bottom. To make matters worse, the cord was also tangled tightly around one leg. In effect, I was hanging upside down, about 20 feet beneath the surface, and out of air—with my buddy out of sight in the darkness. I lunged hard against the cord, and one of the connections broke, plunging me into darkness but freeing me to speed to the surface. In addition to acquiring a good diving light, I now always carry a sharp knife.

Last summer we took our boat, the JUNE Q, through the Willamette Falls navigation locks and started working our way back up river toward the Butteville site. We now have the metal detection equipment to complete the search we started years ago: a Salvagemaster unit that can be operated from the boat by lowering the loop on a cable, a little hand-held underwater

Amphibian for close searches, and a standard land model for checking along the bank.

Our thought was to explore a few other locations along the way, but our plans went awry. One area, Canemah, was so fascinating that we spent most of our available time there.

Canemah means "Canoe Place" in the local Indian language, and it was the place where travelers heading down the Willamette took their canoes out to portage around the thundering cascade. White settlers were also forced to tie up their boats at the canoe place until the navigation locks were completed in 1872. Even after this event, Canemah continued as a small steamer port. The evidences beneath the waters were fascinating.

With the metal detectors, we found in the mud a brass padlock marked "O.&C. R.R.," ornate brass gaslight fittings, a cast-iron toy car, telegraph equipment, and other objects. The diving also yielded many interesting glass and pottery bottles.

As generous as the river has been to us, we do not intend to limit our diving there. Salt water locations have just as many, if not more, thrilling places to explore. For instance, at Port Townsend, Washington, about a hundred yards out in the bay and an equal length south of Union Wharf, lies a floor safe. One side is ripped open, but not clear to the strongbox; the door was knocked off to accomplish that. It apparently reached its resting place via a dock that extended into the harbor. The dock had held various businesses before collapsing in the 1930s. Had the safe been thrown there on some dark night after a "safe job," or had it been deposited there by the collapse of the dock and later opened by a salvage diver?

In either case, it intrigued us, for a burglar could have thrown away anything identifiable, and an early diver in primitive equipment might well have dropped small objects. After finding the safe, we went back for the metal detectors but had no way of marking the precise location. When we returned with the equipment, our units began locating other objects of interest from the collapsed dock: artillery shell casings, silverware, copper sheathing fallen from some hull, and an advertising cut of a "Model '29 Overland." The last time I saw the safe it was being used as a home by a rockfish; we still haven't fully explored it. I have since, however, tucked a Pelican marker-recovery float into the pocket of my buoyancy-compensator vest so I can readily return to objects I have found.

Some of the other places for future exploration have fascinating stories connected with them. Several years ago, a fisheries biologist, Darrell Demory, while on a routine survey of Whale Cove, Oregon, found a full bottle of Scotch whiskey wedged between the rocks. We knew that Smuggler's Rock at the entrance to the cove had been so named because a Prohibition-era rum-runner vessel hit it and sank. This new discovery caused us to look into the matter some more. What a tale we uncovered!

Whale Cove had been a regular smuggler port during Prohibition days. Perhaps Prohibition nights would be more appropriate, for nighttime was when the activity took place. In 1932 the coastal highway still had a number of ferries at major river crossings. The ferries didn't operate at night, so the coast highway was deserted after darkness settled. Smugglers were quick to perceive this, and to note that Whale Cove had a 30-foot-deep channel angling into the deceptively shallow-appearing cove. Adequate depth could be found to reach a bluff where stately fir trees served as a ready-made derrick base. Thus, on the night of Feb. 7, 1932, the SEA ISLAND, out of Victoria, B.C., was heading in toward the two lanterns hanging in the tree, showing the channel and signaling "the coast is clear."

Unfortunately, the channel was not safe that night. A large swell was running, and as the vessel followed the course that took her at an angle to the waves, a large one lifted her and slammed her against the boulder that protrudes from the end of the reef forming the south edge of the entrance. A fire started in the engine room with the same blow that smashed a hole in the hull. Both wounds appeared fatal, so there was nothing the crew could do but abandon ship.

As the vessel settled to the bottom of the cove, she started a chain of events that would lead to a futile effort to salvage the cargo at low tide, seizure of the liquor, and capture of the crew. The quiet that followed was broken by a gangland-style jailbreak and raid to regain the liquor from the jail storeroom, a night chase through the coastal hills, with a spectacular capture of gang, crew, and contraband by Oregon State Police troopers. During the raid, some witnesses reported seeing a green coupe with gangsters carrying submachine guns. If it existed, it was never seen again, either during the chase or since. It is the one remaining mystery of the saga.

The cargo that was seized, stolen in the raid, then recaptured consisted of 51 drums, 3 barrels, and 275 cases of whiskey. This was not all that the SEA ISLAND carried into Whale Cove, however. Partying beachgoers waded and swam in the surf of the cove for weeks, recovering and consuming what salvors and sheriff deputies had missed. Eighteen days after the wreck the sheriff raided the beach again, confiscating another 14 cases of whiskey.

I wonder how much more must be around the bones of the SEA ISLAND. It would be a worthy discovery, for the bottle Darrell found contained whiskey that was still palatable. (I know; I sampled it.) The cork was intact, marked "H & S Special" (Hoyt & Son distillery in Scotland).

Whale Cove is only one of many locations we would like to explore further. Another that has promise is Willow Point near Campbell River, British Columbia. Fred Rogers, author of *Shipwrecks of British Columbia*, first told me of the place. For some reason, not many others are aware of the potential, as little information could be gleaned from residents of the area. However, it is the site of the wreck of the liner, COTTAGE CITY. The vessel was a wooden passenger liner of 1,885 tons, built in Bath, Maine, in 1890, and brought to the Northwest nine years later for the gold-rush trade. It was under the flag of the Pacific Coast Steamship Company when it hit shallow-water rocks in January, 1911. The hull was eventually refloated, but not before a severe storm swept away the superstructure, bridge, and tall black smokestack. Nothing remained above the main deck.

We hoped to find some of the brass portholes and other fixtures at Willow Point. It had taken Fred several days of diving to find the wreckage, but he eventually discovered enough to make the effort worthwhile. Time was short when I tried to repeat his adventure, and although we drifted through the area several times, intrigued by the large ling cod that inhabit the undercut tables of bedrock, we found no wreckage. We weren't in the right location.

At Port Townsend we found a large floor-model safe out in the bay. It had a hole blown in the side, and was occupied by a black rock-fish. Our intent was to return with the Amphibian metal detector and search the surrounding area for coins and jewelry that a burglar might have disposed of as identifiable. However, we became sidetracked along the way by an artillery shell casing, silverware, rifle ammunition, and a zinc advertising cut of a model '29 Overland.

RIVER SALMON SEINE.

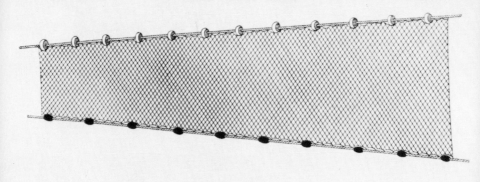

TRUE TAPER.

Average length, feet	300 to 4
Depth, tapered end, feet	16
Depth, shore end, feet	8
Size mesh, inches	4
Size thread	15, 18, 21 or

Excerpt from a Pacific Net & Twine catalog shows the construction of salmon nets in use in the rivers during the early decades of the 20th century. Cork disc floats are shown here, though double-tapered oval wooden floats were common. Large lead weights through which the lower line (lead-line) passes appear black in the illustration. Smaller, closer-spaced leads were also popular.

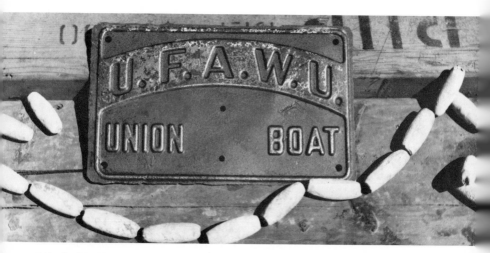

Only the bead-like weights of the lead-line remained of this salmon net in the Nehalem River. The brass United Fishermen & Allied Workers Union boat identification plate was recovered from Quathiaski Cove, British Columbia.

At Willow Point, we were using our light inflatable boat and outboard, letting it drift with us but having one diver holding a tow line so it would stay close. At the end of the drift it was his chore to climb into the boat and pick up the others. We have a portable Digi-Depth 3 depthfinder that we sometimes take along in the inflatable to locate the mass of a wreck, but at Willow Point there was no remaining hull.

Locations like these wreck sites may yield a wealth of maritime relics, or nothing. However, some adventures start out as wreck dives and turn into other profitable undertakings. We were trying to locate the remains of a steamer that burned and sank in Gig Harbor, Washington, when we came upon some old bottles and the only crockery whiskey jug I have ever found intact under water.

On another occasion, finding an old wreck in Nehalem Bay, Oregon, eventually led us to a bonanza of glassware and other relics. What happened was that an individual claimed in a newspaper article to have "identified" our wreck as something we knew it was not, and our reaction sent us on a thorough search of the rest of the bay. We not only found the wreckage of what he said our find was, but stumbled upon a veritable relic hole at the former dock of the town of Nehalem. An amazing number and variety of old bottles and collectables came from that hole.

We should have known to look there, anyway, for places like abandoned docks have been some of our best sites for bottle collecting. In great-grandfather's time, as now, refuse of paper, cans, and bottles accumulated from a crowd. Nearby householders were also prone to bring the family garbage over and drop it off the wharf. After all, there were no anti-litter campaigns then, and in rural areas, seldom any garbage service. The paper and cans have long since deteriorated and disappeared, but the now very collectable glass remains.

Our process of finding bottles, then, has been one of pinpointing where people gathered to work, or perhaps to catch the local ferry. In fresh water, rows of rotting piling provide a clue. Docks normally had close-set rows in a pattern parallel to the water's edge, while piling driven to prevent bank erosion—and no indication of a potential relic-diving site—was closer together, often a single row and perpendicular to the water flow. However, a double row of close-set piling in a V-shaped pattern has often led us to an old ferry site. This was our only indication of the former landing at Brinnon, Washington, for the access road was hidden in trees and undergrowth.

In most saltwater locations, the really old docks, where the most valuable bottles await, have been eaten away by borers. (Technically, borers do not eat wood; they rasp their way into the relatively soft material for protection. Nor are our Northwest borers true teredos. They are of the same family, Teredidae, but the common borers of the Northwest are *Bankia sp.* True teredos are found farther south on the California coast.) The remaining clues for the diver are irregularities on the shore, like approach roads, jetty work, or evidence of dredging. Any piling remnants would be in the high-tide zone where drying kills the borers, and flush with the silt of the bottom, which suffocates them.

Our quest for interesting places to dive has taken many fascinating turns. Nothing seems to enhance the pleasure of the searches, and the discoveries, as much as knowledge of the history associated with a location. It was by chance that we came upon the wealth of information at the Lincoln County Historical Museum. We had been diving at Yaquina City, a former seaport up the bay from Newport, Oregon, but the diving had been only mediocre. Then, quitting early one afternoon, we stopped by the museum, more as something to do, and were shown fine old photographs of the railroad yards, ferry terminal, and dock location we had been seeking. Sailing ships lay at anchor in a readily identifiable area. From then on, the diving was more productive and more fun. The bottles coming from the depths represented those tossed from a floating saloon, from a departing ferry, or dropped from the deck of a schooner awaiting its turn at the dock. In return, we donated a share of the discoveries to the museum.

Since that time I have found other historical societies to be more than willing to share information, usually asking nothing in return. However, it has always been my policy to share, and I hope others will do the same.

I am sure future adventures will take us back to the rivers as well. Bob Upson, in passing on to me the story of early Portland garbage being burned on the back at a site near the Upson houseboat, started a search that not only led to the discovery of the Chinese relics at Sauvie Island, but general interest in the Columbia-Willamette system. One phase that we have not followed up is the early salmon fishery.

Many former commercial fishermen are still around who remember the days of sail in Columbia River fishing boats. At that time, the dock and mooring facilities of the lower Columbia were on the Washington side of the river, for the best fishing was along the north side—a long way from Astoria in a small sailboat. Today those facilities are deserted and fallen down. In the dwindling industry, power boats have replaced sail. Now there are vessels large enough to cross the river quickly even in stormy weather, then to move on to other waters where commercial salmon fishing is still feasible.

Other old-timers remember when commercial fishing was still practiced in the coastal streams. As we were working our way along the muddy bottom of the Nehalem River we came upon the remains of two old commercial fishing boats. One was designed for sail; the other appeared to have been fitted with an outboard motor. Of their nets, all was rotted and swept away except the lead-line that held the lower edge close to the bottom of the river.

While it was Bob Upson who got us started poking around the Columbia-Willamette system, it was Norma Upson, with her collection of log dogs, who got us also paying attention to the relics of log rafting. Although rafting is continuing to a limited degree, there are many older sites where steaming locomotives puffed onto riverbank trestles to drop their loads—places where piling is rotting away and vegetation is beginning to claim the brow logs over which the sawlogs made their splashing entry into the river. At a few of these, the close-set circles of timber show where water towers once stood to fill up thirsty steam engines.

In some cases the rafting coincided with port use. At the Doernbecker landing, a mill had been the principal attraction.

After several instances of stumbling upon interesting underwater locations and having trouble returning to them later, the author always carried a Pelican Marker-Recovery float in the pocket of his buoyancy compensator vest. It consists of a hollow plastic spool which is counterbalanced with a spiked anchor. Pulling a pin releases the anchor, sending the spool to the surface, trailing 120 feet of 225-pound test line.

The Salvagemaster is a dual-purpose metal detector. It can be used by a diver, as shown above, for very precise study of a site. Lynda (left) holds the loop ready to take below, hearing responses through an earphone; Paulette (right) serves as technician in the inflatable boat, making any needed adjustments. Another method is to lower the loop from the boat, then dive only reactive sites. (*Diver Magazine* photo)

Here we found an old cant hook, several peaveys, and axes dropped by pond workers and rafters. Log dogs (iron loops that end in a spear point for log attachment) were abundant, and to our surprise, many turned out to be hand forged. I knew there was a ready market for boom chains that we occasionally came upon, but it was not until Roy Harwood offered to trade nautical relics for the peaveys, axes, and other rafting relics that I realized the value of what we had occasionally passed up.

The former port of Canemah had been a rafting ground after the other river traffic had ceased. We had grumbled about the sinker logs as we searched the river for relics, but later came to recognize that we were being well repaid with axes, log dogs, chains, and hooks. The dogs had been so abundant that when Norma Upson said she could use a few, we jokingly dumped about a hundred at her doorstep.

Albany, Oregon, was the most productive river location for collecting rafting tools. In fact, the first plunge from the boat brought me right back up with an axe in each hand. As we drifted with the current we found more axes, a peavey, and numerous log dogs. The most fascinating object in the channel at Albany, though, was a huge deck winch. We speculated that a raft under tow had become snagged, the tugboat skipper had given full throttle in an attempt to tear it free, but, instead, the winch had been ripped out of the deck.

In a way, the winch on the bottom was a predictor of the end of the story, for within a few months we had worked our way down to the river below Portland and had found where the old tugboats have died. Near the spot where the wheelhouse of the JAMES W juts sadly above the edge of the river, I blundered onto the wreckage of another tug with a long history of service in the lumber industry, the GEO M. BROWN. It was built in 1900 as the GEO R. VOSBERG for the Wheeler Lumber Company.

Pieces of wrecked towboats are scattered along the bank below the BROWN and the JAMES W., and there are rumors of more on the river floor. Some of our next dives will be in the tug graveyard.

INDEX

179

INDEX OF BOTTLE EMBOSSING